Jenny Bristow's Today & Everyday Cookbook

Jenny Bristow's Today & Everyday Cookbook

Gill & Macmillan

Published in Ireland by
Gill & Macmillan Ltd
Goldenbridge
Dublin 8
with associated companies throughout the world
Text © Jenny Bristow 1993
Photographs © Robert McKeag Studios, Coleraine 1993
0 7171 2141 0
Index compiled by
Helen Litton
Print origination by O'K Graphic Design, Dublin
Printed by
ColourBooks Ltd, Dublin

A catalogue record is available for this book from the
British Library.

1 3 5 7 6 4 2

*I dedicate this book with love to my dear mother and late father who made every
day something special when I was growing up.*

Contents

Preface

The Today & Everyday Cookbook is my no-nonsense approach to cooking, with recipes and ideas that are neither complicated nor expensive.

Like so many others, I neither have the time for nor do I enjoy fussy or time-consuming cooking. Yet today, more than ever, we want real food for everyday. This book aims to bring back that relaxed love of cooking which has been on the decline, thus preserving a vital element of home making and family life.

As always, I like to use the best local ingredients combined with old traditions. Many dishes are family favourite recipes, handed down and handed on, altered, adapted and amended as is the wont of every cook. The modern trend for lighter, fresher food so often means streamlined preparation, using only the simplest kitchen appliances and a pinch of imagination—the greatest asset of any cook.

This book is organised into categories ranging from good beginnings to grand finales, finger lickin' chicken recipes to snappy dishes for fish and many simple recipes on how to sauce up food. There are cakes you can bake as fast as you please and many healthful breads.

My roots are firmly set in the country and where the opportunity arises I use the fruits of the hedgerows. What could be tastier than an orchard chicken casserole, home-made blackberry and apple pie, bramble jelly thickly spread on home-made bread, or delicately flavoured jam made from little wild strawberries.

In writing this book I have had much help and encouragement. I would like to thank first my friends and colleagues at Ulster Television who have supported me in this venture, and the crews with whom I work to produce so many of these recipes on UTV 'Live at 6'. A special word of thanks to my producer and director, Ruth Johnston, who never fails to be a source of great inspiration to me. It is a joy that we share the same vision of and approach to cooking and good food.

Robert McKeag and Howard Ward, both artists in their own right, I thank for their patience and excellent photographs. We did enjoy the picnics but not until the photographs were taken.

Thanks to Martha Anderson for typing my every word and for her amazing ability to decipher my writing; she kept the pressure on me as deadlines approached.

My grateful thanks to Cameron's of Ballymena, Anne Osborne, the Quilted Goose, her brother Scott Anthony, The Temple of Flora, Dorothy Hayes, Joanne Hughes, Claire Shiells, Maisie Duncan, Sea Fish Authority, Potato Marketing Board, Maud Hamill, and my many friends at Calor Gas.

Finally, this book could not have been written without the total support and consideration of my husband Bobby, a great lover of good food, and my children who continue to support and sample my many culinary ventures.

Conversion of Measurements

The following equivalents were used in converting between metric and imperial measurements:

Temperature

240 °C	475 °F	regulo 9
230 °C	450 °F	regulo 8
220 °C	425 °F	regulo 7
200 °C	400 °F	regulo 6
190 °C	375 °F	regulo 5
180 °C	350 °F	regulo 4
160 °C	325 °F	regulo 3
150 °C	300 °F	regulo 2
140 °C	275 °F	regulo 1
120 °C	250 °F	regulo ½
110 °C	225 °F	regulo ¼

Volume

3.4 L	6 pints	2.75 L	5 pints
2.25 L	4 pints	1.7 L	3 pints
1.4 L	2½ pints	1.1 L	2 pints
850 ml	1½ pints	570 ml	1 pint
425 ml	¾ pint	380 ml	⅔ pint
280 ml	½ pint	200 ml	7 fl. oz
170 ml	6 fl. oz	140 ml	¼ pint/5 fl. oz
115 ml	4 fl. oz	70 ml	⅛ pint

Weight

1.35 kg	3 lb	900 g	2 lb
680 g	1½ lb	450 g	1 lb
400 g	14 oz	340 g	12 oz
285 g	10 oz	225 g	8 oz
200 g	7 oz	170 g	6 oz
140 g	5 oz	115 g	4 oz
85 g	3 oz	70 g	2½ oz
55 g	2 oz	45 g	1½ oz
30 g	1 oz	15 g	½ oz

1 *Good Beginnings*

For me the starter is the most important part of any meal as it sets the atmosphere for what is to follow. Often this course causes great difficulty, trying to find an alternative to egg mayonnaise, a chilled melon boat or a daring prawn cocktail.

I try to make starters which are appealing, both in appearance and taste, and so often the well-used ingredients require nothing more than a change of sauce or dressing.

Bitter sweet cocktails combines prawns, grapes and pineapple in a sauce which is neither bitter nor sweet. Try serving the sauce separately and allow your guests to help themselves. Smoked mackerel pâté makes a very informal starter as it is ideal to spread on hot buttered toast and served before sitting down at the table. Aromatic prawns are attractive, colourful and impressive with the meat of the prawns turning a delightful coral and white on cooking. Lovely served with dips or on a starter dish garnished with a little salad.

If, like me, you like a hot starter, then granary eggs are delicious. If asparagus is expensive or out of season, substitute with a little spring onion or leeks. Another hot favourite is hot bacon soufflé with sun-dried tomato sauce. Soups are always popular and for early summer, courgette and lemon soup is delicious, especially with the flavour of fresh basil leaves added just before serving. Pumpkin bonfire soup is great for autumn and has the novelty of being served in its shell and garnished with crusty cheese croûtons.

I have included new ideas for melon and grapefruit, those most useful of fruits when a starter is expected in minutes.

I like to keep servings small and even ramekin dishes can be bought in a variety of sizes. The use of colourful garnishes and a little imagination makes such a difference to any starter.

Pied Piper Soup

Here is a soup as hot as you can stand—simply vary the spices according to your taste. A good soup for a really cold day.

1 dessertsp. oil
2-3 teasp. curry powder
½ teasp. turmeric powder
2 cloves garlic
2 onions, chopped
115 g (4 oz) red lentils ⎫
115 g (4 oz) green lentils ⎬ steeped for 2 hours in cold water
2 stalks celery
1.1 L (2 pints) vegetable stock, approximately
140 ml (¼ pint) coconut milk
2 dessertsp. parsley

Heat the oil in a pan and add the curry and turmeric and cook for 1 minute. Add the crushed garlic, onion, drained lentils, celery, stock, and cook in a covered pan for at least 1 hour. This soup can be served chunky but I like to blend it in a food processor. Return the blended soup to the saucepan, add the coconut milk (now readily available in shops), reheat gently and serve garnished with chopped parsley.

Serves 6-8

Courgette and Lemon Soup

This popular vegetable has endless uses but I feel one of the best recipes I have tasted is this courgette and lemon soup. Use fresh basil if available. If not, substitute with parsley.

1.35-1.80 kg (3-4 lb) courgettes
2 large onions, finely chopped
115 g (4 oz) butter
Juice of 1 lemon
1.1 L (2 pints) well-flavoured vegetable/chicken stock
Pinch of paprika
Salt and pepper
1 dessertsp. cream
6 fresh basil leaves or 2 dessertsp. chopped parsley
**   and lemon rind to garnish**

Sweat the onions in the melted butter with the lid on the pan over a low heat for 5-6 minutes. Prepare the courgettes by topping and tailing. If liked, peel them although this soup will have a more superior colour if they are left unpeeled. Finely slice the courgettes, add to the onion, toss in lemon juice and sweat for a further 15 minutes until soft.

Add half the stock and the seasoning and simmer until all the vegetables are soft. Transfer to a food processor and whizz until the vegetables become smooth. Return to the saucepan, add the remainder of the stock and season to taste. Heat through for a further 5 minutes. If necessary, adjust the consistency of the soup by adding more stock.

Just before serving, add the cream and coarsely chopped fresh basil—this adds such a fragrant flavour to this soup—and lemon rind to garnish. If fresh basil is not available, substitute with parsley. Serve hot.

Serves 8-10

Pumpkin Bonfire Soup

This is an ideal dish for Halloween. The colour, texture and flavour of this soup all depend on the ripeness of the pumpkin; otherwise the dish will be tasteless. It can be quite a novel idea to serve the soup in the pumpkin shell itself.

1 pumpkin, 2.70-3.15 kg (6-8 lb)
1 large onion, peeled and chopped
15 g (½ oz) fat
70 ml (⅛ pint) white wine
1.1 L (2 pints) good chicken stock
280 ml (½ pint) milk
Salt and black pepper
Pinch of nutmeg
Pinch of paprika
280 ml (½ pint) cream

To prepare the pumpkin cut the top off, remove the seeds carefully, then scoop out the flesh from the inside. This is much easier to scoop out than a turnip. Leave less than 1.25 cm (½ in.) of flesh on the inside of the pumpkin if using it as a tureen. Dice the pumpkin.

Next, cook the diced onion in the melted fat, allow to sweat for 1-2 minutes before adding the pumpkin flesh. Cook over a low heat, stirring well, for a further 5 minutes. Next add the white wine and simmer for a further 10 minutes. Add the stock and milk and allow the soup to simmer gently for 10-15 minutes. Liquidise or sieve the soup and return to the pan. Add the

3

seasoning, then the cream and allow to simmer gently before serving. This soup can be returned to the pumpkin shell and kept hot in a pre-heated oven at 180 °C (350 °F or regulo 4). Serve with toasted cheese croûtons.

Serves 8-9

Aromatic Prawns

340 g (12 oz) raw prawn tails
Pinch of chilli powder
1 teasp. fennel seeds
3 cloves
5 black peppercorns
2.5 cm (1 in.) piece cinnamon stick
2 tablesp. sunflower oil
2 cloves garlic, chopped
1.25 cm (½ in.) piece root ginger, peeled and finely chopped
1 small onion, finely chopped
3 tomatoes, skinned and chopped
1 tablesp. water
1 tablesp. white wine vinegar
2 teasp. dark brown sugar
Salt and pepper
Coriander leaves to garnish

Place the chilli powder, fennel seeds, cloves, peppercorns and cinnamon stick into a shallow pan. Dry fry for 1-2 minutes to release the flavour. Cool, then crush the spices to a powder in a plastic bag using a rolling pin. Heat the oil in a shallow pan, cook the garlic, ginger and onion for 2-3 minutes. Add the spices, cook for a further 2 minutes. Stir in the tomatoes and water, cover and simmer for 5 minutes. Add the vinegar, sugar, prawns, and the seasoning. Cover and cook for about 5 minutes or until the prawns are pink in colour. Garnish with coriander leaves and eat hot with your fingers.

Serves 3-4

Smoked Mackerel Pâté

This recipe proves that fish is one of the simplest and least complicated foods to cook. This dish can be made in minutes with smoked mackerel either peppered or plain. An ideal dip, starter or good on hot buttered toast.

225 g (8 oz) smoked mackerel
55 g (2 oz) low-fat mayonnaise
55 g (2 oz) fromage frais
Salt and pepper
Pinch of paprika
1 teasp. chopped dill or parsley

Peel the skin off the mackerel, and using a fork, flake the fish into a bowl with the mayonnaise, fromage frais, seasoning and the finely chopped dill or parsley and mix well. If using as a starter transfer to individual small ramekin dishes and chill in the fridge.

Serves 3-4

Mango and Melon with Raspberry Sauce

1 small melon, peeled and cut into chunks
2 mangoes, peeled and cut into chunks
450 g (1 lb) fresh raspberries
2 tablesp. icing sugar, sieved
Sprigs of applemint to garnish

Place the peeled and chopped melon and mangoes in a bowl, cover and allow the flavours of the two fruits to marinate for at least 1 hour.

Prepare the sauce by rubbing the raspberries through a fine sieve. Add the sieved icing sugar.

Put the mangoes and melon into shallow glasses, spoon a little of the sauce over them and garnish with sprigs of variegated applemint.

Serves 4-6

Melon in Rosemary Syrup

Melon is such a useful starter and the rosemary syrup transforms this fruit completely. Try serving the melon piled back into the shells if using the smaller varieties such as Galia, and dust with a sprinkling of demerara sugar.

1 melon, cut into small cubes

Syrup
280 ml (½ pint) water
2 tablesp. freshly chopped rosemary
30 g (1 oz) caster sugar
30 g (1 oz) demerara sugar
Sprigs of rosemary to garnish

In a small saucepan heat the water, chopped rosemary and caster sugar to boiling point. Continue bubbling for at least 5 minutes then strain the syrup and allow to cool. Add the cubed melon to the syrup and leave to infuse for at least 1 hour or if time permits, in a covered bowl overnight. Serve in some pretty glasses or return to the melon shells, sprinkle with demerara sugar and serve chilled, garnished with sprigs of rosemary.

Serves 4

Bitter Sweet Cocktails

Fruit cocktails are always popular for starters but this one combines the sweetness of fruit and prawns with the sharpness of the sauce.

225 g (8 oz) peeled prawns
8 pineapple chunks, cut in half
115 g (4 oz) black grapes, cut in half
115 g (4 oz) green grapes, cut in half
3-4 lettuce leaves, finely shredded

Sauce
4 dessertsp. mayonnaise
4 dessertsp. Greek yoghurt
Few drops Tabasco sauce
Juice of ½ lemon
Salt, pepper, pinch of paprika
1 teasp. finely chopped herb such as dill or parsley

Place the shelled prawns, pineapple and grapes in a bowl. Toss together and leave covered to marinate. Prepare the sauce by mixing mayonnaise, yoghurt, Tabasco sauce, lemon juice, seasoning and herbs together. Add the prawns, pineapple and grapes, toss around and serve in separate glasses with a little shredded lettuce around the glasses.

If preferred, the sauce can be served separately.

Serves 3-4

Toasted Grapefruit

2 large, ripe grapefruit
2 teasp. cinnamon
2-4 tablesp. demerara sugar

Cut grapefruit in half and loosen the segments with a sharp knife, then liberally sprinkle with demerara sugar and cinnamon. Place under a hot grill until hot and bubbling. Serve hot or cold.

Serves 4

Granary Eggs

4 hard-boiled eggs
8 slices of granary bread
30 g (1 oz) butter
Pinch of mixed herbs
115 g (4 oz) shelled prawns
225 g (8 oz) fresh asparagus, lightly steamed
Wedges of lemon and a little grated Parmesan cheese to garnish

Sauce
15 g (½ oz) butter
15 g (½ oz) flour
280 ml (½ pint) milk or half milk/half white wine
115 g (4 oz) Parmesan cheese
Pinch of salt and pepper

Butter the granary bread and sprinkle with a little mixed herbs. Arrange in an ovenproof dish with half a hard-boiled egg set on top of each slice. Slice the egg lengthways. Scoop out the yolk, mix with a little knob of butter and 30 g (1 oz) of the finely chopped prawns. Return to the egg whites, piling well on top.

Arrange the lightly steamed asparagus over the eggs, sprinkle with prawns and pour the white sauce over the top. This is a traditional white sauce which has the cheese added just as it comes to bubbling point. Sprinkle a little of the remaining cheese over the top and flash under the grill until golden-brown and bubbling. Serve hot.

Serve 4

Hot Bacon Soufflé with Sun-dried Tomato Sauce

Sun-dried tomatoes are definitely the flavour of the month. They have been around for quite a long time but are now appearing in profusion on our supermarket shelves. They add such flavour to these little hot baked soufflés which can be served with the sauce spooned over the top or separately.

Serve in individual ramekin dishes.

Soufflé
55 g (2 oz) cooked, diced bacon
55 g (2 oz) butter
30 g (1 oz) plain flour
280 ml (½ pint) milk
85 g (3 oz) grated or crumbled cheese
½ teasp. paprika
Salt and pepper
70 ml (⅛ pint) yoghurt or fromage frais
3 eggs, separated

Sun-dried Tomato Sauce
2 tablesp. olive oil
2 crushed cloves garlic
½ onion, very finely chopped
1 fresh small tomato, finely chopped
1 spring onion, very finely chopped
30 g (1 oz) soft brown sugar
2 tablesp. sun-dried tomatoes, shredded
Vegetable stock or water (optional)

First prepare the sun-dried tomato sauce. Place the olive oil in a small saucepan, add the garlic, onion, chopped tomato, spring onions, sugar and finally the shredded, sun-dried tomatoes. Simmer gently for 6-7 minutes until the sauce becomes well blended. If required, thin the sauce with 2-3 dessert-sp. of vegetable stock or water. This sauce will hold while making the soufflé.

To make the soufflé: first make a white sauce using the butter, flour and milk, add the diced, cooked bacon, crumbled cheese, paprika, salt, pepper, fromage frais or yoghurt and egg yolks. Mix well together, then fold in the well-beaten egg whites. Mix gently, then transfer to the lightly greased ramekin dishes and bake in the oven at 200 °C (400 °F or regulo 6) for 15-20 minutes until well risen and cooked. Serve immediately with the warmed sauce.

Serves 4

Cheese Logs

With sheep and goat's cheese becoming widely available this makes a very different starter. Serve with strips of radicchio lettuce or curly endive.

4 sheets filo pastry
30 g (1 oz) melted butter
4-5 leaves of lightly steamed spinach
4 pieces of cheese, approx. 4.5 cm (1½ in.) in length
4-5 leaves basil, coarsely chopped
Salt and pepper
1 egg, lightly beaten

Roll out the filo pastry sheets and brush with melted butter, then lay the sheets on top of each other. Lightly steam the spinach for 2-3 minutes and remove the centre stalk. When cool, place over the pastry as if making a swiss roll. Divide the pastry evenly into 4 squares. On each one place a piece of cheese approximately 4.5 cm (1½ in.) in length, sprinkle with the salt and pepper and a little chopped basil.

Roll up the pastry into individual logs, brush them with beaten egg and bake in the oven at 200 °C (400 °F or regulo 6) for 10-15 minutes. Serve hot.
Serves 4

Garlicky Lemon Chicken Wings

This makes a very tasty first course. You can exchange the wings for drumsticks giving a more substantial luncheon dish. Good served with a fresh green salad and granary bread.

12 chicken wings
2 tablesp. sesame oil
3 garlic cloves, crushed
Rind and juice of ½ lemon
1 teasp. paprika
Salt and freshly ground black pepper
1 small carton of yoghurt

Wash and dry the chicken wings. I like to cut off the ends as there is little eating on them. Score the wings with a sharp knife so that the marinade can penetrate. Brush with a little oil. In a bowl place the crushed garlic cloves, lemon rind and juice, paprika, seasoning and yoghurt. Mix well, then add the chicken wings. Toss around, then cover and leave in a cool place for at least 1 hour to allow to marinate. Drain the wings, place on a baking sheet and bake in the oven at 180 °C (350 °F or regulo 4) until crunchy and nicely golden-brown. These wings also cook well under the grill and are ideal for the barbecue.

Serves 3-4 as a starter

Sizzling Chilli Chicken

2 chicken breasts, cut into fine strips

Marinade
2-3 tablesp. sherry
Salt and pepper
1 dessertsp. soy sauce
1 green chilli, finely chopped
1 clove garlic, crushed
1 tablesp. hazelnut or walnut oil
1 dessertsp. red, sweet chilli sauce
2 dessertsp. toasted sesame seeds

Prepare the marinade for the chicken pieces by mixing the sherry, seasoning, soy sauce, very finely chopped chilli and crushed garlic together in a bowl. Add the ribbon-sliced strips of chicken and leave to marinate for at least half an hour. In a frying pan or wok heat the oil, add the drained pieces of chicken and cook quickly. Add the marinade and chilli sauce to the pan and cook on high heat for a further 2 minutes, allowing the chicken pieces to become crispy and golden.

Drain and serve with a little tossed salad and dust with toasted sesame seeds.

Serves 4

Spinach with Brie in Filo Pastry

The Brie for this recipe should not be over-ripe. Serve as a starter or light luncheon dish with a crisp green salad.

225 g (8 oz) spinach leaves
225 g (8 oz) Brie cheese
225 g (8 oz) filo pastry
1 egg, lightly beaten

The quantities depend on the number of servings required. Roll out the filo pastry into a square approximately 15 cm x 15 cm (6 in. x 6 in.). Arrange two young steamed spinach leaves and a good-sized cube of Brie cheese on top of each one.

Brush the edges with beaten egg, then gather up the pastry shaping into dainty-sized parcels. Bake at 190 °C (375 °F or regulo 5) for not longer than 5 minutes.

Serves 4

Cold Stuffed Tomatoes

3 plump tomatoes
1 tablesp. chopped basil or parsley
55 g (2 oz) grated cheese, mildly flavoured
55 g (2 oz) brown rice, cooked
1 teasp. wholegrain mustard
1 clove garlic, crushed
2-4 dessertsp. natural yoghurt or fromage frais
Lettuce leaves, sprigs of basil to serve

Scoop the insides out of the tomatoes after removing the lids. Finely chop the tomato purée and add the parsley, cheese, rice, mustard, garlic and yoghurt. Mix lightly, then return to the tomatoes. Place the lids on top and serve on a bed of lettuce lightly garnished with sprigs of basil or parsley.

Serves 3

2 *Fowl Play*

C hicken has to be one of the most popular and versatile meats on our supermarket shelves today. Its popularity must lie in the fact that it is such a convenient food, low in fat, cooks speedily, can be served hot or cold and is available in many different forms.

Chicken breasts on or off the bone have endless uses. I much prefer to buy them off the bone as there is no wastage and they are so easy to prepare. Chicken thighs are good value and very juicy. Drumsticks, although they have a slightly tougher meat, are loved and enjoyed by children and adults alike. Wings are not renowned for their bulk but if cooked correctly make wonderful starters such as with chilli or marinated in garlic and lemon. Roast chicken is a firm family favourite in many a home, especially on Sundays, but it can be made more flavoursome if a little butter is rubbed on the breast of the chicken under the skin before roasting. Another tip I use is to turn the bird upside down in the roasting tin after cooking and at least 10 minutes before serving to allow the juice to flow back through the flesh.

Good home-made chicken stock is easily made and can transform soups, stews and casseroles or simply form the basis of many a good sauce.

Chicken nowadays appears in many guises on menus worldwide, from coq au vin to English roast chicken. I have included many of our tried, tested and loved recipes from the meal-in-a-bowl chicken and sweetcorn soup, to St Clement's chicken, a tangy chicken dish served with a refreshing sauce and fresh fruit salad. There's also orchard chicken, a really substantial main course dish where drumsticks or breasts can be used depending on the budget.

Orchard Chicken Casserole

Casserole dishes are great standbys for families as they need little supervision. At Halloween add a little chopped pumpkin to this dish to enhance the flavour and colour.

2-3 chicken fillet breasts or 6 drumsticks
1 dessertsp. oil
1 large onion
4 rashers of lean back bacon, diced
115 g (4 oz) mushrooms, sliced
2 large apples, cut into large wedges
4 potatoes, peeled and cut into large chunks
570 ml (1 pint) stock
140 ml (¼ pint) cider
1 teasp. mixed herbs

In a heavy-based pan, cook the onion, diced bacon and sliced mushrooms in the oil, stirring well. Add the apple pieces and cook for a further 2 minutes. Transfer to an ovenproof dish. In the same pan, lightly brown the chicken on both sides. I like to cut the fillets up into approximately 8 pieces and this should take 4-5 minutes to brown evenly. Transfer the chicken pieces to the ovenproof dish with the onions, bacon, mushrooms and apple. Add the wedges of uncooked potatoes and any remaining juices from the pan. Pour the stock, cider and seasoning over the chicken. Cover lightly and bake in a pre-heated oven at 180 °C (350 °F or regulo 4) for about 1 hour or until the chicken is tender. This dish can also be cooked successfully on the hob or in a microwave.

Serves 4

Crusty Chicken Casserole with Cheese Soufflé

The crusty cheese soufflé topping gives a rather unusual finish to this casserole. The unique flavour of the sheep's cheese is excellent, although if you prefer to use your standby cheese from the fridge then this dish will work equally well.

450 g (1 lb) chicken pieces
1 dessertsp. oil
4 rashers of mild-flavoured bacon, chopped
115 g (4 oz) mushrooms, finely sliced
1 onion
2 shallots
2-3 stalks of celery
Pinch of paprika and black pepper
1 tin condensed chicken soup
140 ml (¼ pint) fromage frais

13

Soufflé Topping
30 g (1 oz) butter
30 g (1 oz) flour
280 ml (½ pint) milk
3 eggs, separated
115-170 g (4-6 oz) grated crumbled cheese (preferably sheep's)
1 extra egg white (optional)
Seasoning

Cook the chicken pieces either in a microwave, by steaming or lightly cooking in a pan. In a separate pan, gently fry the bacon, mushrooms, onion and shallots in the oil. Add the chicken to the vegetables, then add the celery (uncooked) and a little seasoning.

The sauce for this dish is made by combining the low-fat fromage frais and tinned chicken soup. Mix well, then add the chicken and the vegetable mixture to the sauce and transfer to a greased ovenproof dish.

Prepare the soufflé topping by melting the butter in a pan, add the flour, seasoning and milk, mixing to a white sauce. Heat until the mixture thickens. Allow to cool before adding the separated, lightly-whisked egg yolks and the crumbled cheese. Finally add the whisked egg whites. If the egg whites are beaten too stiffly, it is difficult to fold them in and retain the volume required for a soufflé. Spoon on top of the casserole—if liked, a little crumbled cheese can be sprinkled on top. Bake at 190 °C (375 °F or regulo 5) for 25-30 minutes until golden-brown, and the soufflé is well puffed up. Serve hot—delicious with a bowl of green salad.

Serves 4-6

St Clement's Chicken

This tangy chicken dish combines grilled chicken breasts with a light refreshing sauce made from fresh orange pieces and celery.

4 chicken breasts
Little oil for brushing

Sauce
1 small onion, finely chopped
1 tablesp. oil
240 ml (½ pint) chicken stock
Juice of 2-3 large oranges

Dash of Worcestershire sauce and soy sauce
1 tablesp. arrowroot, blended with a little cold water
2-3 oranges, cut into segments
2 sticks celery, cut in pieces

Brush the chicken breasts with oil and grill on both sides for 4-5 minutes, depending on the thickness of the breasts.

To make the sauce, lightly cook the finely chopped onion in a little oil for 1-2 minutes. Add the chicken stock, freshly squeezed orange juice, dash of Worcestershire sauce and soy sauce and blended arrowroot. Bring the sauce to boiling point and stir for at least 1 minute until the sauce becomes clear. Add the orange segments and celery pieces, heating through. Serve hot or warm with the chicken breasts. As an alternative to rice or pasta, try serving this chicken with a tangy fruit salad made using seasonal fruits marinated in their own juices (kiwi, oranges, mangoes and apples).

Serves 4-6

Nutty Chicken

This attractive casual dish, almost Chinese yet with local influences, has that wonderful stir-fry look with brown glazed nuts, onion strips, sprinkled with peppers and undertones of being garlicky, hot and satisfying. Serve with honey-toasted baked potatoes.

450 g (1 lb) chicken pieces
2 medium onions
2 tablesp. vegetable oil
2 cloves garlic, crushed
½ red pepper
½ green pepper
1 bunch spring onions, cut into fine strips
115 g (4 oz) roasted hazelnuts or filberts
30 g (1 oz) unsalted cashew nuts
Salt and black pepper
1 dessertsp. tomato purée
Chicken stock (if needed)

Cut the chicken into fine strips. Cut the onions into good-sized pieces, approximately 1.5 cm (½in.). Heat half the oil in a large pan or wok and toss the onions until lightly browned, then add the garlic and cook for a further minute. Transfer to a dish. Pour the remaining 1 tablesp. of oil into the heated pan, add the chicken and cook over a high heat, turning until browned, tender and cooked. To the chicken add the peppers cut into strips, spring onions, roasted hazelnuts, cashew nuts, seasoning and tomato purée. A little chicken stock may be added to avoid the chicken sticking to the pan. Toss for about two minutes to allow the flavours to mix. Transfer to a heated serving dish and serve at once.

To roast the hazelnuts or filberts, crack the shell off the nuts and place on a baking sheet in the oven at 180 °C (350 °F or regulo 4) for about 10 minutes. They can also be roasted under a grill but will require careful attention.

Serves 4

Spicy Chinese Chicken with Special Fried Rice

A light spicy chicken dish with that unique Chinese flavour and the crunch of vegetables. Be careful not to overcook this dish as the textures will be spoiled.

Marinade
2 dessertsp. soy sauce
2 dessertsp. sherry vinegar
1 teasp. grated root ginger
1 tablesp. brown sugar
Pinch of salt
Pinch of Chinese Five Spice Powder

450 g (1 lb) chicken pieces, cut into ribbon strips
2 dessertsp. sesame oil
1 small onion, chopped
½ red pepper, cut into chunks
½ green pepper, cut into chunks
1 small tin of water chestnuts
2 dessertsp. spring onions, coarsely chopped
1 dessertsp. chilli sauce
1 vegetable stock cube
1 dessertsp. cornflour
140 ml (¼ pint) water
Spring onions and toasted sesame seeds to garnish

Place the ingredients for the marinade in a large bowl. Mix together and add the chicken cut into ribbon strips. Leave to marinate for at least 1 hour if possible.

Heat the sesame oil in a wok until a faint blue haze appears. Add the drained chicken pieces and cook rapidly for 4-5 minutes until golden-brown and lightly cooked. Drain the chicken onto a plate. Reheat the oil, then add the prepared vegetables, water chestnuts and finally the spring onion. Only a quick cooking is required here, tossing around in the hot oil for 1-1½ minutes. Then return the chicken pieces. Mix well before adding the stock ingredients—chilli sauce, stock cube and cornflour blended with the water and, if needed, a little seasoning. A little pinch of Chinese Five Spice Powder may again be added at this stage. Heat through until the cornflour thickens the sauce. Continue to cook for 2-3 minutes and serve hot, sprinkled with finely chopped spring onions and toasted sesame seeds.

Spring onion curls can also be used to garnish this dish. They can be prepared simply by cutting two-thirds of the way down through about 5 cm (2 in.) strips of spring onion, making approximately 6-8 cuts. Place in iced water for approximately half an hour until the stems begin to curl. Dry well before serving.

Serves 4

Special Fried Rice

A variety of rices can be used for this dish—Patna, wholegrain or Basmati to name but a few, each producing a very different result. The addition of extra vegetables can add extra colour.

340 g (12 oz) rice, cooked and cooled
2 dessertsp. sesame oil
2 eggs, lightly beaten
450 g (1 lb) cooked, peeled prawns
½ teasp. grated green ginger (optional)
6-8 shallots, finely chopped
2 dessertsp. soy sauce to flavour
Little seasoning

Cook the rice in a large saucepan. I find one of the secrets in cooking rice is to keep it constantly on the boil. A little salt can be added during cooking. Drain, ensuring it is very dry. If cooked rice is being kept for several days, it is important to store it in the fridge.

Heat the oil in a wok and when a faint blue haze appears, add the lightly beaten egg, and whisk into the oil while it continues to cook; this should not take any longer than 1 minute. Add the rice to the wok, tossing well and then finally add the soy sauce, prawns, ginger, shallots and a little seasoning. Heat through, then serve.

Serves 3-4

Persian Rice with Chicken

Pari, a great friend and wonderful cook, first introduced me to this aromatic and lightly perfumed Persian rice dish. The colour, flavour and texture are very different and ideal to serve with pork and chicken dishes. Finely shredded chicken can be added to this dish before serving.

12-15 tangerine oranges to make the peel
Water to cover peel, approx. 570 ml (1 pint)
3 glasses water/570 ml (1 pint)
900 g (2 lb) granulated sugar
450 g (1 lb) Basmati rice
1.1 L (2 pints) boiling salted water
4-5 stamens saffron
1 tablesp. boiling water
115 g (4 oz) blanched almonds, shredded
115 g (4 oz) pistachio nuts, shredded

Prepare the tangerine peel by removing the outer peel from the oranges, then carefully remove any white pith with a sharp knife. Cut the peel into fine shreds; this is a lengthy process but well worth the effort. Place the peel in a heavy-based pan with sufficient cold water to cover. Bring to the boil and cook for 15-20 minutes, leave to cool. Then drain off the water, fill the pan again with cold water and repeat the process. After draining for the second time, leave the peel in the pan, add 3 glasses of water (about 1 pint) and 900 g (2 lb) sugar and boil until the liquid reduces by half. Leave to cool.

Prepare the rice, washing several times to prevent it breaking during cooking. Add the rice to a pan with 2 pints of boiling salted water and leave to boil for 8-9 minutes. Prepare the saffron by placing the threads in a small bowl with 1 tablesp. of boiling water; leave to infuse for 6-7 minutes at least. When the rice is almost tender, drain off any excess water and return to a very low heat. Using the end of a wooden spoon, make holes in the rice to allow the steam to escape. Mix gently with the saffron, shredded almonds, pistachio nuts, 4-5 tablesp. of shredded peel and a little of the syrup. Serve hot. Cooked shredded chicken can also be added at this stage. This dish can be served as a main course.

Serves 6

Chicken in Sweet and Sour Orange Sauce with Boiled Rice

450 g (1 lb) chicken pieces
2 dessertsp. honey
1 dessertsp. soy sauce
Salt and pepper
1 small onion
2 sticks celery
140 ml (¼ pint) chicken stock
Juice of 2 large oranges
1 dessertsp. arrowroot, blended with the chicken stock
2 tablesp. ginger wine
Orange segments
2 tablesp. cranberries
8-9 kumquats
2 dessertsp. olive oil
Grated orange peel (optional)
Pistachio nuts (optional)

Cut the chicken breasts into evenly-sized pieces. Place in a bowl and leave to marinate for at least 1 hour with the honey, soy sauce and seasoning.

Next cook the chicken. In a large shallow pan, heat the oil, lightly fry the onion and celery, then add the chicken pieces and cook well. Remove from the heat, then add the blended chicken stock, orange juice, arrowroot, ginger wine and simmer gently for 5-6 minutes. Just before serving, add the orange segments, sliced kumquats, cranberries and if liked a little grated orange peel and pistachio nuts. Serve bubbling hot with rice or pasta.

This is a lovely dish to serve at Christmas time when the cranberries are plentiful, but it makes an ideal dish at any time of the year by exchanging the cranberries for another seasonal fruit such as mangoes.

Serves 4

Boiled Rice

Cooking rice causes many people great difficulty, yet there is no great secret to successful fluffy rice. Each variety of rice on the market today requires a special treatment and cooking time. However the most commonly used is Patna rice.

340 g (12 oz) Patna or long grain rice
½ teasp. salt
570 ml (1 pint) boiling water

Put a large saucepan of water on to boil, add the salt and when it comes to full rolling boil, add the rice gradually so the water does not go off the boil. Allow the rice to boil uncovered for 10-12 minutes. I find it better to leave the lid off during cooking. When ready, the grains should be tender, having absorbed the liquid but if not, drain any excess water from the pan and serve immediately. The most common cause of sticky rice is water not boiling rapidly during the cooking process. Should the rice become sticky, pour into a colander and wash under the cold tap after cooking. Re-heat the rice by pouring boiling water over it and serve.

Serves 4

Golden Chicken Risotto

225 g (½ lb) chicken
15 g (½ oz) butter
2 tablesp. olive oil
1 large onion, finely chopped
225 g (8 oz) sliced mushrooms
225 g (8 oz) Basmati or Patna rice
570 ml (1 pint) chicken stock
Salt and pepper
2 yellow peppers, cut into strips
4 dessertsp. lightly whipped cream or yoghurt
1 teasp. wholegrain mustard
Rind and juice of 1 orange
2 dessertsp. finely chopped parsley

Cut the chicken pieces into evenly-sized strips, then fry gently in the pan with the olive oil and butter mixed until lightly golden-brown. Remove the chicken from the pan. Add the onion and sliced mushrooms, cooking for 2-3 minutes until opaque but lightly cooked. Add the rice, and cook

Pumpkin bonfire soup

Bitter sweet cocktails

Nutty chicken

Chicken drumsticks with mustard and whiskey sauce

Orchard chicken casserole

River-bank sea trout with roasted sesame seeds

Grilled mackerel with gooseberry and elderflower sauce

Foiled pork parcels

Caramelised sliced potatoes with garlic and chives

Barbary duck breasts with rhubarb and redcurrant sauce

Slemish lamb with a high-spirited sauce

Bread and butter pudding

*Winter/summer
strawberries*

Elderflower syllabub

through for 2-3 minutes before adding the chicken stock and seasoning. Bring to simmering point and cook for approximately 8 minutes. Add the sliced peppers, place cooked chicken on top of the rice, cover and simmer for a further 2-3 minutes until the chicken is tender and the rice grains have absorbed all the liquid.

In a separate bowl mix the lightly whipped cream or yoghurt, mustard, orange juice and rind and pour over the top of the rice and chicken. Toss gently, then serve sprinkled with parsley.

Serves 4

Chicken Drumsticks
with Mustard and Whiskey Sauce

This is an ideal dish for the barbecue season. This sauce can either be served warm or cold but it is one which improves in flavour if made up in advance and stored in the fridge.

4-6 chicken drumsticks or breasts
2 dessertsp. olive oil
Salt and finely ground black pepper

Sauce
115 ml (4 oz) Greek yoghurt
2 teasp. wholegrain mustard
Rind and juice of ½ lime or orange
2-3 tablesp. Bushmills whiskey
1 dessertsp. honey
Salt and pepper
Bunch of thyme and 2 dessertsp. finely shredded orange peel
  to garnish

Brush the drumsticks or breasts with oil and season well. Cook either on the barbecue, under the grill or in the oven until golden-brown and well cooked. Cooking time depends on size but I feel it is important to ensure chicken in any form is well cooked. Make the sauce by mixing yoghurt, mustard, honey, whiskey, fruit juice and rind together and adjust the seasoning. It can be heated a little before serving but do be careful not to overheat; otherwise the consistency will become thin. Garnish with thyme and finely shredded orange peel.

Serves 4

Honey and Cider Baked Chicken

Every time I cook this chicken dish I vary the flavour according to the herbs in season at the time. Coriander, tarragon and thyme add just that hint of individuality to this chicken dish. Baking is one of my favourite no-nonsense methods of cooking without the necessity for split-second timing that puts every cook on edge.

900 g (2 lb) chicken pieces
2 dessertsp. honey
Few drops soy sauce
4 dessertsp. cider
1 dessertsp. oil
30 g (1 oz) butter
1 small onion, finely chopped
570 ml (1 pint) cider
Little herbs for flavour—tarragon, thyme, coriander
140 ml (¼ pint) soured cream
Salt and freshly ground pepper
115 g (4 oz) celery pieces
4 spring onions, finely chopped
3 crisp eating apples, cored and thickly sliced

Marinate the chicken pieces in the honey, soy sauce and 4 dessertsp. of cider. Leave aside covered for at least 1 hour to allow the flavours to blend.

In a pan heat the oil and butter, lightly fry the onion until soft but not coloured. Remove to a lightly greased ovenproof dish. Next cook the chicken pieces a little at a time until lightly browned all over, and place on top of the onion. Pour the cider over the chicken and onion and add the herbs. Bake slowly at 180 °C (350 °F or regulo 4) for ¾-1 hour until tender, depending on the size of the chicken pieces, basting with the cider during cooking.

Remove the chicken from the oven and using a slotted spoon, arrange on a serving dish. Pour the cooking liquid into a saucepan and boil rapidly to reduce. Cool slightly, then add the cream and seasoning. Add the celery and spring onions.

This sauce can be slightly thickened by blending the cream with 15 g (½ oz) flour. If the liquid is too warm when the cream is added the sauce may be too thin.

In a separate pan fry the apple wedges gently in the remaining butter for no longer than 1 minute. Pour the sauce over the chicken, garnish with apple wedges and sprigs of herbs.

Serves 6-8

Coriander and Chicken Bake

Herbs combine well with chicken, and coriander, tarragon and rosemary are my favourites.

Quick, speedy and tasty toppings are always useful when cooking for the family and this topping is made using peanuts and wholemeal flour.

340 g (12 oz) cooked chicken pieces

Topping
115 g (4 oz) shelled peanuts, finely chopped
55 g (2 oz) wholemeal flour
55 g (2 oz) mozzarella cheese
6-8 leaves coriander, finely chopped or 1 teasp. dried coriander

Sauce
30 g (1 oz) fat
30 g (1 oz) plain flour
280 ml (½ pint) milk or half milk half cream
140 ml (½ pint) stock
2 teasp. wholegrain mustard
3-4 spring onions

Prepare the topping by mixing in a bowl the finely chopped peanuts, wholemeal flour, mozzarella cheese and finely chopped fresh coriander leaves. If these are not available then use 1 teasp. of dried coriander.

Cook the chicken pieces either by steaming in a microwave or in a pan with a little oil. Do not overcook the chicken at this stage as it will be cooked further in the sauce.

Make the sauce by melting the fat in a saucepan and add the flour, milk and stock. Cook over a gentle heat for 1 minute until the sauce becomes smooth and glossy. Add the mustard and the finely chopped spring onions. To obtain the best flavour, I like to sauté the onions first in a little oil.

Place the chicken pieces in an ovenproof dish, pour the sauce over them, sprinkle the topping over the sauce and bake at 190 °C (375 °F or regulo 5) for 20-25 minutes until golden-brown and bubbly.

This makes a very tasty casserole dish with an interesting flavour.
Serves 4

Chicken and Sweetcorn Soup

570 ml (1 pint) chicken stock
2 large tins sweetcorn, 400 g (14 oz)
225 g (8 oz) cooked chicken pieces
115 g (4 oz) lightly cooked mushrooms
2-3 finely chopped spring onions
Pinch of salt
2 dessertsp. chopped parsley

Make the chicken stock (alternatively chicken stock cubes may be used). Add the sweetcorn to the heated stock, simmer for 8-10 minutes, then liquidise. This greatly improves the texture of this soup. Add the cooked chicken pieces, mushrooms, spring onions and seasoning, allowing to simmer for 5 minutes. Sprinkle with parsley and serve hot with crusty bread.

The quantities of chicken pieces and mushrooms can be increased to give this very tasty soup a much chunkier consistency.

Serves 4-6

Sunday Roast Chicken

Sunday is one of the most relaxed times to cook, and roast stuffed chicken has to be one of my favourite dishes, using a well-brought-up chicken and an interesting stuffing. Roasting is the most uncomplicated method of cooking and requires no split-second timing.

1.35-1.80 kg (3-4 lb) free range chicken
1 lemon
30 g (1 oz) butter
280 ml (½ pint) chicken stock or stock and white wine mixed

Stuffing
225 g (8 oz) medium oatmeal
2 dessertsp. olive oil
1 large onion, finely chopped
1 stalk celery, very finely chopped
30 g (1 oz) nuts, preferably pine or pistachio
30 g (1 oz) melted butter
Salt and a little white pepper
55 g (2 oz) brown breadcrumbs

Few sprigs of fresh tarragon or ½ teasp. dried
1 egg yolk

Honey-roasted potatoes, seasoned steamed vegetables
  (buttered leeks, broccoli) to serve

To prepare the stuffing, lightly roast the oatmeal on a baking sheet in the oven or under a pre-heated grill. This will intensify the nutty flavour of the oatmeal. Heat the oil in a frying pan, lightly fry the very finely chopped onion and celery. Cook slightly before adding the nuts, melted butter, roasted oatmeal, seasoning, breadcrumbs, tarragon and finally the egg yolk to bind the stuffing together.

Pack the neck of the bird with the stuffing, pat down well and secure the neck flap underneath. Smear the breast of the chicken with butter, moisten with the juice and rind of the lemon, sprinkle with salt and pepper and place on foil in a roasting dish. Chicken is traditionally dry roasted, but I prefer the French method of cooking with butter and lemon juice, then surrounding the chicken with stock or wine and using this to baste during cooking. This helps to keep the bird moist. Cook at 200 °C (400 °F or regulo 6) for 20-25 minutes. Reduce temperature to 190 °C (375 °F or regulo 5) for 20 minutes per lb weight of bird.

To test if it is ready, pierce the thickest part of the thigh with a skewer. If the juices run clear the chicken is ready. Serve with some lightly steamed vegetables and use the juices to make gravy.

Serves 4-6

Snap Crackle Chicken

This pie has a wonderful combination of flavours and textures. Aubergines lack flavour so try grilling them lightly coated with oil instead of frying.

450 g (1 lb) chicken fillets, cut in strips
1 aubergine
2 dessertsp. olive oil
1 egg, lightly beaten
115 g (4 oz) Parmesan cheese, grated
2 onions, sliced
2 cloves garlic, crushed
400 g (14 oz) tin tomatoes
Salt and pepper

Wash and slice the aubergine thickly, then blanch in boiling water for 1 minute only. Drain and pat dry. Brush each slice with a little oil and brown under a hot grill for a few minutes. Next prepare the chicken fillets. Cut the chicken into strips, season with salt and pepper, coat with lightly beaten egg, toss in grated Parmesan cheese, dusting off the excess cheese.

In a shallow pan lightly fry the chicken pieces on both sides. Drain on absorbent paper. In a separate pan fry the onion slices with the crushed garlic cloves for several minutes, then add the tinned tomatoes and cook for a further 2 minutes. Pour into an ovenproof dish. Arrange overlapping layers of chicken and grilled aubergine on top. Sprinkle with Parmesan cheese and cook in the oven at 190 °C (375 °F or regulo 5) for 25-30 minutes until the chicken is well cooked and golden-brown.

Serve piping hot with Mother McKeag's bacon muffins.

Serves 4

3   *Hook, Line and Skillet*

At a time when eating trends are moving more towards animals that either fly or swim, it is reasonable to assume we are cooking and eating more fish. There is a new wave of enthusiasm for fish as we become more healthy in our attitude to food and see how good it actually is for us. Fish has such a lot going for it. It is low in fat, low in cholesterol, and oil-rich fish especially helps to regulate the viscosity of our blood. It is a food which is good for the brain and generally high in protein, vitamins and minerals. The versatility of fish is ideal for cooks. Many of these recipes combine the simplest of approaches with imagination and ingredients which complement the fish's own flavour.

I am a fish lover, as thankfully is my family, so the choice of fish for us often just depends on the catch of the day or what is freshest and best.

Plaice with oranges is refreshing and the tangy flavour of the citrus fruits brings out the best in the fish. Smoked fish crumble makes a good economical family meal. Whiting, one of our most common fish, can come to life with the addition of a tangy leek, lime and butter sauce. A good substantial fish chowder can turn a soup into a meal if served with crusty bread, and salmon with pasta gives an instant meal, one I reckon you will remember and try over and over again.

My love affair with fish has been going on for many years, from catching sticklebacks in the stream with a jam pot at the age of four to deep sea fishing off the coast of Portstewart, catching anything from eels to mackerel. Now I find myself cooking trout in the pan at midnight—the ones my son catches on his evening expeditions.

Freshness is so important in the cooking of fish. Ideally, cook the fish the day you buy it, or—even better—catch it!

Kipper Cakes

450 g (1 lb) kipper fillets (fresh or defrosted) skinned
1 egg, beaten
Dash of Worcestershire sauce
170 g (6 oz) fresh breadcrumbs

Place the kipper fillets into a food processor or blender. Process or blend until finely flaked. Stir in the egg, Worcestershire sauce and breadcrumbs. Divide the mixture into 8 pieces and shape into 5 cm (2 in.) rounds. Chill for 10-15 minutes. Cook under a low grill for 8-10 minutes, turning once. Serve with salad and tomato or onion relish.

Smoked mackerel fillets can be used in place of kipper fillets.

Serves 4

Traditional Seafish Pie

450 g (1 lb) white fish, skinned and cubed
125 g (4 oz) peeled prawns
30 g (1 oz) butter or margarine
225 g (8 oz) leeks, sliced
30 g (1 oz) flour
280 ml (½ pint) milk
Salt and pepper
Pinch of nutmeg
450 g (1 lb) cooked potatoes
200 g (7 oz) tin of carrots, drained

First, preheat the oven to 200 °C (400 °F or regulo 6). Then melt the butter or margarine in a pan and cook the leeks for 2-3 minutes. Stir in the flour and cook for 1-2 minutes. Remove from the heat, gradually stirring in the milk. Return to the heat and cook, stirring until the sauce has thickened. Add the fish, prawns and seasoning. Spoon into a large ovenproof dish. Mash the potatoes and carrots, season with salt, pepper and nutmeg. Spoon or pipe the potato mixture over the fish. Bake for 35-40 minutes. Serve with a selection of green vegetables.

Serves 4-5

Plaice with Oranges

4 x 170 g (6 oz) plaice or whiting fillets, skinned
15 g (½ oz) butter or margarine
285 g (10 oz) tin of mandarin oranges (in natural juice), drained
1 tablesp. lemon juice
Pinch of cayenne pepper (optional)
Salt and pepper
30 g (1 oz) flaked almonds or chopped mixed nuts, toasted
Chopped parsley to garnish (optional)

Roll the fillets from head to tail, skinned side inside, and arrange in a shallow ovenproof dish. Dot with butter or margarine and spoon the mandarin oranges over the fish. Sprinkle with lemon juice, cover and bake at 190 °C (375 °F or regulo 5) for 20-25 minutes. This dish is also suitable for cooking in the microwave. Leave to stand covered for 2 minutes. Season, sprinkle with the almonds and cayenne pepper.

Garnish with parsley before serving with mashed potatoes and green vegetables.

Serves 4

Monkfish with Bacon

680 g (1½ lb) monkfish tails, cut into cubes
225 g (8 oz) mildly-flavoured bacon or gammon
1 dessertsp. cooking oil
Juice of ½ fresh lemon or lime
140 ml (¼ pint) dry white wine
140 ml (¼ pint) fish or vegetable stock
1 spring onion
Pinch of salt, pepper and paprika
2 grapefruit, cut into segments
280 ml (½ pint) cream, lightly whipped
Crushed pink peppercorns and watercress to garnish

Prepare the monkfish tails by cutting the fish into good-sized chunks. Cook the ribbon strips of bacon in a little oil; the secret of success in this dish is the texture of the crispy bacon combined with the fish. Next add the cubes of fish and continue cooking for 3-4 minutes, tossing gently. Add the juice of half a freshly squeezed lemon or lime, white wine, fish stock, spring onion and seasoning, tossing well. Reduce the temperature slightly and add the grapefruit segments and finally the lightly whipped cream. Be careful to reduce the temperature or the cream will become very thin and spoil the consistency of the sauce.

Serve hot, garnished with pink peppercorns and watercress.

Serves 4-6

Dinner Party Salmon Pasta

There is no substitute for cream in this recipe and it will enhance your favourite fish. I find salmon both colourful and especially suitable for this dish.

285 g (10 oz) pasta shapes
450 g (1 lb) fresh salmon, cut into large chunks
2 spring onions, finely sliced
1 dessertsp. oil
280 ml (½ pint) cream
115 g (4 oz) mozzarella cheese
Pinch of paprika and black pepper
2 dessertsp. chopped dill or parsley
Lemon twists to serve

Cook the pasta shapes in boiling salted water for about 8-9 minutes. Add sufficient water to cover the pasta—the addition of 1 teasp. of oil to the water will prevent the pasta sticking together. Do not allow the pasta to overcook. Gently cook the salmon pieces either in a microwave or by steaming for 4-5 minutes until pale pink and cooked. Cook the spring onions in the oil to improve their flavour and colour. This should take approximately 1 minute.

Place the cream in a saucepan or in a bowl over a pan of warm water. Be careful not to allow the cream to become too hot. Add the grated or cubed cheese and allow to melt in the cream. Add the seasonings, herbs, spring onions. Return the cooked salmon to the sauce and heat through. Serve poured over the hot pasta and garnish with dill and lemon twists.

Lightly steamed leeks or sliced, cooked Jerusalem artichokes may also be added to this dish before serving.

Serves 4

Chunky Fish Chowder

This is probably our family's favourite fish soup. It's often difficult to persuade children that fish is good for them as well as good for their brains! This chowder combines mildly-flavoured fish with chunky vegetables and creates a soup with a wonderful texture.

450 g (1 lb) smoked haddock or cod
450 g (1 lb) fresh white haddock or cod
450 g (1 lb) freshly shelled prawns (optional)
1 large onion, finely chopped
450 g (1 lb) potatoes, cut into chunks
1 leek, cut into rings
2 stalks celery
1 green pepper
115 g (4 oz) freshly shelled garden peas
55 g (2 oz) butter
280 ml (½ pint) fish or vegetable stock
280 ml (½ pint) milk or half milk/half cream
Salt, pepper, pinch of paprika
Fresh dill or parsley

Prepare the vegetables. Chop the onion finely, cut the potatoes into good-sized chunks, slice the leeks, celery, pepper and shell the peas. Remove any bones from the fish and cut into bite-sized pieces. In a large saucepan melt the butter, lightly cook the onions, peas, leeks, celery and pepper for 1-2 minutes.

Next add the potato pieces and continue to cook for a further 2 minutes. Add 280 ml (½ pint) fish or vegetable stock and continue simmering for 10-15 minutes until the potatoes show signs of softening. Add the cubed fish, prawns, seasoning, milk and/or cream and cook gently until the fish is tender. Add the sprigs of dill or parsley, heat through and serve.

This is a meal-in-a-bowl soup, filling and nutritious. Serve with crusty bread.
Serves 6

Whiting Fillets
with Leek and Lime Butter Sauce

This recipe shows how a sharp tangy sauce can change an every-day fish. The sauce is equally good with salmon or trout.

4 x 115 g (4 oz) fillets whiting
30 g (1 oz) flour
30 g (1 oz) butter
1 dessertsp. oil

Sauce
3 spring onions/shallots, finely chopped
115 g (4 oz) butter
140 ml (¼ pint) white wine
Juice of 1 lime
1 small leek, finely sliced and lightly steamed
2 dessertsp. lightly whipped cream
Sprigs of herb, dill or parsley and finely shredded strips
of lime to serve

Dust the whiting fillets with flour and fry in a pan with oil and butter mixed. Cook for 3-4 minutes on either side and turn once. Drain on kitchen paper and keep warm while making the sauce.

In a separate pan cook the shallots in half the butter for 1 minute. Remove from the heat, add the white wine and bubble for 1-2 minutes. Next add the remaining butter and whisk well. Add the lime juice and leek. Turn off the heat and add the cream. A little finely chopped herb can also be added.

Garnish with lime and herbs and serve warm with the fish fillets.
Serves 4

Whole Baked Sea Trout with Roasted Sesame Seeds

The flavour, texture and aroma of this fish require nothing more than to keep it simple.

1 trout, approx. 900 g (2 lb)
140 ml (¼ pint) dry white wine
Juice of 1 lemon
Sprinkling of sea salt
Knob of butter
55 g (2 oz) sesame seeds

Ask your fishmonger to prepare and clean out the fish if you don't feel like beheading and gutting it yourself. Rinse the fish well on the inside and pat it dry. Sprinkle the inside of the cavity with sea salt and lemon juice. For a simple stuffing bake a mixture of 115 g (4 oz) chopped mushrooms, 1 teasp. chives and half a chopped onion inside the cavity. Make 2-3 diamond slashes along the length of the fish, place in foil, dab with butter and pour the dry white wine over the top. Seal and bake in the oven at 200 °C (400 °F or regulo 6) for approximately 25 minutes. Cooking time depends very much on how well you like your fish cooked. Transfer to an oval platter, sprinkle with sesame seeds roasted under the grill and serve hot.

Serves 2-3

Filo Fish Pie

I find a fish pie is always popular and filo pastry is light and easy to work with. Filo pastry is now readily available in the supermarket and the choice of fish in this pie can vary depending on the budget or the selection available in the fishmongers.

680-900 g (1½-2 lb) seafood—salmon, trout, prawns, lemon sole, turbot, whiting, scallops—cut into bite-sized pieces

Sauce
55 g (2 oz) butter
140 ml (¼ pint) fish stock
115 g (4 oz) finely sliced leeks
140 ml (¼ pint) dry white wine
280 ml (½ pint) whipping cream or milk
Pinch of cayenne and black pepper
15 g (½ oz) flour blended with 1 dessertsp. water
225 g (8 oz) filo pastry sheets
1 egg, beaten
Sesame seeds

Cook the fish in the melted butter for 2-3 minutes. If smoked fish such as trout is included it will not require cooking, just heating through.

Remove the fish from the pan and make the sauce. Add the fish stock to the melted butter remaining in the pan and next the finely sliced leeks, cooking for 1-2 minutes. Add the white wine, lightly whipped cream, cayenne and black pepper and blended flour and cook until bubbling gently. Do not overcook or the sauce will become thin. Return all the fish to the pan, stirring very gently for 1 minute. Leave to cool.

In a pie dish arrange 2 sheets of the filo pastry overlapping at the sides. Pour the cooled fish mixture into the pie, arranging the remaining pastry on top.

I like to divide up each sheet into 4 pieces, and arrange them in an overlapping fashion on top of the pie, ensuring the fish mixture is well covered.

Brush with beaten egg, sprinkle with sesame seeds and bake in the oven at 200 °C (400 °F or regulo 6) for 20-25 minutes or until golden-brown and bubbling. Serve hot.

Serves 4-6

Crusty Puffed Fish

The delightful sauce used in this recipe adds style to even the simplest of fish dishes and any white or pink-fleshed fish is ideal. I like to serve it well-puffed up and golden-brown with grapefruit segments dusted with cinnamon and brown sugar flashed below the grill until bubbling.

450 g (1 lb) fish (salmon, trout, plaice, cod, haddock or whiting)
2 dessertsp. lemon or lime juice
Salt and pepper
15 g (½ oz) butter

Sauce
4 dessertsp. low calorie mayonnaise
1 dessertsp. (of your favourite) sweet relish
¼ teasp. paprika
1 dessertsp. finely chopped parsley
2 egg whites, stiffly beaten

Prepare the fish by cutting into good-sized strips, then place in a shallow ovenproof dish. Season and sprinkle with lemon juice and a little butter. Cook either in the microwave or bake in the oven at 190 °C (375 °F or regulo 5) until almost cooked, approximately 10-15 minutes. The thickness of the fish will affect the cooking time.

While the fish is cooking, make the sauce. Mix together the mayonnaise, relish, seasoning and parsley, then gently fold in the stiffly-beaten egg whites. Spread this over the fish and continue cooking in the oven for a further 6-7 minutes until golden-brown and risen. Serve at once.

Serves 4

Caribbean Spiced Fish with Saffron Rice

Here is a dish which brings back the flavours of those holidays spent abroad. After all, food is often the hidden agenda on many holidays and this dish conjures up the aromas of far away places using fish, chilli, coconut, mangoes and pineapple.

680 g (1½ lb) red snapper
1 dessertsp. oil
Juice and zest of 1 lime and 1 lemon
1 teasp. mustard seeds, crushed
1 teasp. cardamom seeds, crushed
1 dessertsp. oil
2 cloves garlic, crushed
1 green chilli, finely chopped
1 small onion, very finely chopped
1 mango, cut into fine slices
2 dessertsp. freshly grated coconut
115 g (4 oz) pineapple cubes
70 ml (⅛ pint) coconut milk
1 dessertsp. mango chutney
140 ml (¼ pint) vegetable stock
1 dessertsp. spring onion

Saffron Rice
225 g (8 oz) Basmati rice
½ onion, finely chopped
1 dessertsp. oil
570 ml (1 pint) boiling water
10 saffron strands
2 dessertsp. hot water

Cut the fish into good-sized cubes and marinate in the oil, lemon and lime juice and zest for at least half an hour. In a separate pan, on a gentle heat, dry roast the crushed mustard and cardamom seeds for at least 30 seconds until the aroma is given off. Add 1 dessertsp. of oil and gently fry the garlic, finely chopped chilli and onion, cooking until opaque—approximately 1 minute. Next add the cubes of fish and any marinade left in the bowl. Cook over a gentle heat until golden and almost cooked. Add the mango, coconut, pineapple, coconut milk, chutney, and stock; stir and leave to simmer gently for 5 minutes until the fish is tender and cooked. Add the spring onions and serve with saffron rice.

Serves 4

Saffron Rice

In a separate pan heat the oil and gently cook the onion for no longer than 1 minute until glistening. Add the boiling water. Stir only once at this stage, then turn down the temperature and allow the rice to cook gently for 9-10 minutes until the grains are tender. Add the saffron strands which have been steeping in hot water for 10 minutes. Toss only once and serve immediately.

Grilled Mackerel with Gooseberry and Elderflower Sauce

Oil-rich fish are becoming more popular with the emphasis on health and the medical advice that these fish should be included in the diet at least twice a week. The combination of gooseberry sauce and mackerel is particularly good.

2 fresh mackerel, cleaned (each approx. 450 g/1 lb)
Little lemon juice

Sauce
115 g (4 oz) fresh gooseberries
1 dessertsp. elderflower cordial
30 g (1 oz) demerara sugar
2 dessertsp. dry white wine
2 dessertsp. water
Lemon twists and dill to serve

Cook the whole mackerel under a hot grill for 4-5 minutes on either side. A little lemon juice can be sprinkled inside the fish before grilling.

To make the sauce, heat the gooseberries, cordial, sugar, wine and water in a saucepan over a gentle heat for 3-4 minutes. Serve with the mackerel.

Garnish with lemon twists and a sprinkling of dill.

Serves 2

Crumbly Baked Cod with Scallions

This tasty and quick fish dish is one of our all-year-round favourites. Vary the fish depending on what is freshest and best and, above all, good value at your fishmonger.

450 g (1 lb) white cod fillets
½ onion, very finely chopped

Topping
2 dessertsp. olive oil
30 g (1 oz) melted butter
2 dessertsp. parsley
1 lemon rind and juice
Salt and pepper
115 g (4 oz) fine white breadcrumbs
55 g (2 oz) grated cheese (optional)
2-3 scallions, finely chopped, to serve

Prepare the fish by skinning and removing any bones. Cut into good-sized pieces and place in a well-oiled ovenproof dish. Next make the topping. Cook the onion in the heated olive oil until opaque, add the butter, parsley, lemon rind and juice, seasoning and breadcrumbs. Cook through over a gentle heat for 1 minute. Spread the mixture over the fish. If using cheese, grate it over the crumbs before baking in the oven at 190 °C (375 °F or regulo 5) for 20-25 minutes. The fish should flake apart easily with a fork when cooked. Serve sprinkled with finely chopped scallions.

Serves 4

4 *Flash Meals with Little Cash*

S o often I have been asked for recipes that are quick, easily prepared, suitable for that evening meal in a rush and most important, ones which will not stretch the budget.

When times get tough, good, healthy, comforting and reasonably-priced food is important. The filler foods such as potatoes, rice and pasta provide the basis for many a nutritious meal. Often only a good sauce to accompany them is all that is required.

Eating healthily on a budget can be quite a challenge and involves a little careful shopping, healthy ways of cooking with reduced fat and plenty of imagination.

Fish crumble is a great dish to make as the range of fish to choose from is so vast. Coley, whiting or cod are ideal in this recipe. Always look for the best buys. Frozen fish is also a good standby.

Potatoes are good value for money and a variety of fillings can be used in potato quiche to accommodate the family likes and dislikes.

Foiled pork parcels are economical to make and an ideal dish if cooking for one or two people. Weekend broth is probably one of the most welcoming, warming and filling soups I know. Full of goodness, it improves on keeping for 24 hours.

Instant burgers are a great standby for children who want a nutritious snack on the table in minutes. When the store cupboard is put to the test, take a tin of tuna with pasta shells—an economical filler which tastes delicious.

Winter Standby

2 potatoes, boiled and grated
½ small onion, finely chopped
2 eggs, lightly beaten
2 dessertsp. milk

Salt and pepper
1 dessertsp. oil
Knobs of butter

Filling
115 g (4 oz) white fish
1 small packet frozen mixed vegetables
1 tomato, sliced, and parsley to garnish

Grate the cooked potatoes into a bowl, add the finely chopped onion, lightly beaten egg, milk and seasoning and mix lightly with a fork. In a shallow pan heat the oil and butter. Add half the potato mixture, spreading out to a pancake shape. Sprinkle the white fish and vegetables on top of the potato mixture and cook over a low heat until the pancake mixture becomes crispy and the fish is cooked. Pour the remainder of the shredded potatoes on top and finish cooking by either placing under the grill or returning to the hob. Cook until a crispy golden-brown.

Serve hot with sliced tomatoes and sprinkle with a little parsley.
Serves 2

Warming Winter Hot Pot

450 g (1 lb) steak pieces
1 dessertsp. oil
1-2 cloves garlic, crushed
2 onions, finely chopped
2 stalks celery
2 carrots, diced
1 leek, sliced
450 g (1 lb) lentils or split peas
½ teasp. paprika
Pinch of salt and pepper
570 ml (1 pint) stock or water
1 dessertsp. tomato purée
225 g (8 oz) mangetout peas, sliced (optional)
¼ shredded Savoy cabbage

Crunchy Baked Potato Slices
4 potatoes, cut into slices
Little oil for brushing
1 egg, lightly beaten
Oregano to sprinkle over potatoes

Cut the steak pieces into even bite-sized pieces, trimming off any visible fat. Toss the meat in the heated oil for 2-3 minutes to seal in the juice and brown evenly. Remove the meat from the pan, then cook the garlic, onion and celery in the oil and meat juices until opaque and lightly cooked —approximately 2-3 minutes. Return the meat to the pan, and add the diced carrot, leek and pulses such as peas and lentils which can be steeped overnight to shorten the cooking time. Add the seasoning, tomato purée and stock. Replace the lid and cook gently for 2-2½ hours. This hot pot can either be cooked on the hob, in the oven or is ideal for a slow cooker.

Approximately 20 minutes before serving add the sliced mangetout peas and shredded cabbage. Replace the lid and simmer.

Serve the hot pot with crunchy baked potato slices. Peel and slice the potatoes, brush with oil and lightly beaten egg. Sprinkle with a little oregano and bake in the oven at 180 °C (350 °F or regulo 4) for about 15-20 minutes.

Serve the crunchy potatoes arranged around the hot pot and sprinkle with freshly chopped parsley.

This hot pot may require a little extra stock to be added during cooking.
Serves 8

Smoked Mackerel and Pasta Bake

450 g (1 lb) smoked mackerel, flaked
225 g (8 oz) pasta shapes
1 tablesp. oil
1 medium onion, finely chopped
3 tomatoes, finely chopped (keep skin on)
1 small tin tomatoes
Little seasoning
½ teasp. oregano (optional)

Topping
55 g (2 oz) oatmeal

55 g (2 oz) muesli
55-85 g (2-3 oz) low-fat cheese, grated
Finely chopped parsley to garnish

Cook the pasta in boiling water for 8-9 minutes until tender. Drain and keep warm. Heat the oil in a pan, add the onion and cook until soft. Next add the finely chopped tomatoes and the tinned tomatoes and cook gently. Add the flaked, smoked mackerel, remembering to remove its skin beforehand. A little seasoning can be added at this stage—oregano is particularly good with smoked mackerel. Finally add the drained cooked pasta to the fish mixture, heat through and transfer to a serving dish.

Make the topping by mixing the oatmeal, muesli and cheese together. Sprinkle over the top of the mackerel dish and grill until golden-brown for 2-3 minutes. Serve sprinkled with finely chopped parsley.

Serves 6

Smoked Fish Crumble

A dish which can be made using cod, haddock, whiting or coley.

225 g (8 oz) white fish - cod, haddock, whiting or coley
225 g (8 oz) smoked fish
225 g (8 oz) broccoli, lightly steamed

Sauce
25 g (1 oz) fat
25 g (1 oz) flour
280 ml (½ pint) milk
Salt and pepper

Crumble
55 g (2 oz) wholemeal flour
55 g (2 oz) white flour
55 g (2 oz) oat bran
55 g (2 oz) polyunsaturated margarine
25 g (1 oz) grated cheddar cheese
1 packet potato crisps
Salt, pepper and paprika

Cut all the fish into good-sized cubes and cook either in a microwave or by poaching gently for 3-4 minutes. Drain and place the fish in a well-greased ovenproof dish, season and arrange the lightly steamed broccoli over the top of the fish. If using frozen broccoli it should not require cooking.

To make the sauce, melt the fat in a saucepan, add the flour and milk, mixing well. Bring to the boil stirring continually. Season to taste and pour over the fish and broccoli.

Make the crumble by mixing all the flours together. Rub in the fat, add the grated cheese and crisps and season. Sprinkle the topping over the fish and bake in the oven at 190 °C (375 °F or regulo 5) for 20-25 minutes.

Serves 6

Potato Quiche

A very easy dish to prepare, especially if you have leftover potatoes.

3 potatoes, cooked
Pinch of nutmeg, salt, pepper
3 eggs
2 rashers cooked bacon
1 onion, finely chopped } **combine**
115 g (4 oz) sliced mushrooms, cooked
70 ml (⅛ pint) milk
55 g (2 oz) chive-flavoured cottage cheese
85 g (3 oz) grated cheese
1 dessertsp. chopped parsley

Mash the potatoes very finely with the salt, pepper and nutmeg. Add 1 egg lightly beaten, mix and spread evenly over the base of a loose-bottomed quiche tin approximately 20-23 cm (8-9 in.) in diameter. Cover the potato base with the bacon, mushroom and onion mixture. If liked, add a little chopped herb at this stage. Prepare the topping by mixing together 2 beaten eggs, milk, finely mashed cottage cheese and half the grated cheese. Pour over the quiche, sprinkle with the remainder of the cheese and bake at 190 °C (375 °F or regulo 5) for 30 minutes until golden-brown. Serve sprinkled with chopped parsley.

Serves 3-4

Foiled Pork Parcels

2 pork chops
1 small onion, finely sliced
2 pineapple rings
½ red pepper, diced
2 potatoes, cut into slices and lightly cooked
140 ml (¼ pint) vegetable stock
Salt and black pepper
1 dessertsp. oil
2 dessertsp. parsley, finely chopped

Gently fry the pork chops for 3-4 minutes on either side, then place each on a rectangular piece of foil. Place on top the sliced onions, pineapple ring, diced pepper and potatoes. Season and cover with stock. Secure the foil parcel and bake in the oven at 200 °C (400 °F or regulo 6) for 35-40 minutes. Serve sprinkled with parsley.

Serves 2

My Mum's Weekend Broth

Good broth needs to be made a day in advance to allow the flavour and texture to develop. Everyone believes their Mum makes the best broth they ever tasted. This is my Mum's recipe which serves anyone who is hungry.

2 large chicken joints
1.7 L (3 pints) cold water
Salt and pepper
2 large onions
2 leeks
2 carrots
2 sticks celery
115 g (4 oz) pearl barley
115 g (4 oz) split peas
115 g (4 oz) lentils
115 g (4 oz) haricot beans
4 dessertsp. finely chopped parsley to serve

Place the chicken joints in a large saucepan with the water and seasoning, bring to the boil and simmer for 10-15 minutes. Most of the scum will come to the surface during this initial cooking. Using a wooden spoon lift off any scum. To the pan add the finely chopped onion, leeks, carrot, celery, barley, peas, lentils and haricot beans. Place the lid on top and simmer gently for at least 2 hours. The pan may require topping up with water as the pulses absorb the moisture.

Re-heat the soup on the second day, add the finely chopped parsley 5 minutes before serving and allow to bubble gently. Adjust the seasoning.

Spicy Vineyard and Yoghurt Chicken

This dish can be turned into a supper dish by the addition of this unusual healthy topping or if preferred, serve the strips of chicken as a light main course with crusty bread and salad.

4 chicken breasts, cut in half
2 tablesp. oil
3 cloves garlic, crushed
1 onion, finely chopped
½ teasp. turmeric powder
½ teasp. paprika
15 g (½ oz) flour
Salt and pepper
280 ml (½ pint) chicken stock
55 g (2 oz) roasted hazelnuts
115 g (4 oz) green grapes
115 g (4 oz) black grapes with seeds removed
1 small carton Greek yoghurt
½ teasp. grainy mustard
1 dessertsp. chopped parsley

Topping
140 ml (¼ pint) natural cottage cheese
1 small carton low-fat yoghurt
1 egg, lightly beaten
55 g (2 oz) grated cheese
Pinch of paprika

Heat the oil in a large heavy-based frying pan. Add the halved chicken breasts and brown on both sides for 2-3 minutes. If serving this dish without the topping, I like to leave the skin on the chicken. Drain the chicken from the pan and add the garlic, onion, spices, flour and seasoning and cook for a further 2 minutes. Add the stock and leave to simmer for 15 minutes. Next add the roasted hazelnuts (cook in the oven or under a grill to bring out the flavour), the grapes cut in half with the seeds removed and finally the yoghurt and mustard blended together. Heat through and serve at this point if not using the topping. Do not allow to boil or the consistency of this sauce will become thin. Serve by sprinkling with freshly chopped parsley.

To make the topping, mix the cottage cheese with the yoghurt, grated cheese and lightly beaten egg and paprika. Spread the topping over the chicken pieces and cook for 10-15 minutes at 200 °C (400 °F or regulo 6) until golden-brown.

Serves 4

Home-coming Casserole

This gentle cooking method for chicken joints is an ideal way of having a hot bubbling casserole ready for eating on returning from shopping. The flavours of chicken, chestnuts, apricots, onion and rosemary slowly combine to create a really tasty casserole with a wonderful aroma to greet you.

4-6 chicken joints
1 large onion, cut into rings
2 dessertsp. olive oil
1 stick celery
1 carrot
115 g (4 oz) apricots
225 g (8 oz) button mushrooms
225 g (8 oz) shelled chestnuts (optional)
450 g (1 lb) small unpeeled potatoes
280 ml (½ pint) chicken stock
280 ml (½ pint) red wine
1 teasp. paprika

Heat the oil in a roasting tin or large ovenproof casserole. Add the onion rings and chicken joints and toss over a gentle heat until well coated and golden-brown. Next add the carrot and celery cut into small pieces and toss in the oil. Add all the remaining ingredients, apricots, mushrooms, shelled chestnuts, scrubbed potatoes, chicken stock, red wine and paprika. Toss around, cover and cook in the oven at 160 °C (325 °F or regulo 3) for a long, slow cooking to allow the flavours to blend, for about 2 hours.

The temperature can be reduced to allow an even longer, slower cooking depending upon the length of the shopping expedition.

Serve piping hot with roasted root vegetables, garlic and honey.

Serves 4

Take a Tin of Tuna

1 large tin of tuna fish (225 g/8 oz approx.)
450 g (1 lb) pasta shells
570 ml (1 pint) boiling salted water and 1 dessertsp. oil
2 teasp. olive oil
1 onion, diced
2 cloves garlic, crushed
115 g (4 oz) sliced mushrooms
1 red pepper, chopped
1 large tin tomatoes (400 g/14 oz)
280 ml (½ pint) vegetable stock
Salt and pepper
3 tablesp. chopped parsley

Cook the pasta shells in boiling salted water and 1 dessertsp. of oil for 7-8 minutes, then drain. In a separate pan heat the oil, add the onion and garlic, cooking until lightly browned. Add the sliced mushrooms and red pepper and continue cooking for 3-4 minutes. Add the tomatoes, stock, salt and pepper and simmer for 10-15 minutes. Finally add the pasta shells and flaked tuna fish. Heat through and serve garnished with parsley.

Alternatively, this dish may be baked in the oven at 190 °C (375 °F or regulo 5) for 15-20 minutes and finished sprinkled with a little grated cheese.

Serves 4-6

Fiery Hot Turkey Salad

This recipe is ideal for turkey pieces after Christmas or perhaps the remains from the Sunday roast chicken. The spices can be varied depending on how hot your family like their food.

340 g (12 oz) cooked turkey, diced
3 sticks celery
4 spring onions, finely chopped
140 ml (¼ pint) mayonnaise
140 ml (¼ pint) fromage frais
2 teasp. cornflour
Juice of ½ lemon
115 g (4 oz) grated cheese
1 teasp. paprika
½ teasp. turmeric powder

Topping
1 packet potato crisps
½ teasp. paprika

The secret of this dish is not to overcook, otherwise the sauce will become thin. Place the first 10 ingredients in a large bowl, mix well then transfer to a greased ovenproof dish. Mix together the crushed crisps and paprika, sprinkling over the chicken dish. Bake in the oven at 190 °C (375 °F or regulo 5) for approximately 15 minutes until hot and bubbling. This dish cooks well in a microwave oven.

Serves 4

Vegetarian Hot Pot

This is a one-pot vegetarian stew using an aromatic combination of spices. A dish which is delicious served with pasta or steamed rice.

1 dessertsp. olive oil
1 onion
2 cloves garlic
1 teasp. cumin powder
1 teasp. coriander powder
1 teasp. curry powder
Salt and pepper
225 g (8 oz) pumpkin or marrow (optional, if in season)
1 carrot, finely diced
2 potatoes
2 red peppers, diced
1 parsnip, finely diced
1 red chilli, finely chopped
1 green chilli, finely chopped
2 x 400 g (14 oz) tins tomatoes
Vegetable stock (if required)

Heat the oil in a large pan. Add the onion, garlic, cumin, coriander, curry powder and seasoning and sauté until soft. Add the diced pumpkin or marrow, carrot, parsnip, potatoes, chilli and peppers and continue cooking until all the vegetables are well coated. Add the tinned tomatoes and, if needed, a little vegetable stock as this liquid will reduce considerably during cooking. Cover and simmer for 30 minutes; adjust the seasoning before serving.

Serves 4-6

My Burgers

450 g (1 lb) lean minced steak
450 g (1 lb) lightly cooked vegetables (carrot, parsnip, onion)
1 dessertsp. finely chopped parsley
1 egg, beaten
Salt and pepper
Little oil to fry

Cook the grated vegetables either by steaming, microwaving or in a pan with a little oil to soften them slightly. This allows the vegetables to combine more easily with the minced steak.

Combine all the ingredients using the egg to bind. Divide the mixture into 3-4 burgers, and shape into rounds. After mixing the raw ingredients and dividing them into round shapes, pop into your fridge for 30 minutes before cooking—this helps the burger keep its shape.

Cook for 3-4 minutes on either side (turning once) and drain on kitchen paper. Serve with a little salad.

Serves 3-4

Instant Burgers

Here are two very quick ideas for a nutritious snack if served with a glass of milk. Each recipe serves 4.

Sweetcorn and Bacon Burgers
1 small tin of sweetcorn (198 g/7 oz)
2-3 rashers of grilled bacon, chopped
1 tablesp. mayonnaise
30 g (1 oz) grated cheese (optional)
4 baps

Mix all ingredients together, spoon on top of 4 lightly grilled baps and heat through either in the oven at 180 °C (350 °F or regulo 4) for 5-6 minutes or flash under a hot grill for 1-2 minutes.

Tuna and Celery Burgers
1 small tin of tuna fish (220 g/8 oz)
1 stalk celery, finely chopped
30 g (1 oz) grated cheese
1 tablesp. mayonnaise
4 baps

Chop the celery finely, mix with tuna fish (or sardines if preferred), add the cheese and mayonnaise, mixing well. Spoon on top of the burger baps and grill for 1-2 minutes. Serve hot.

Festive Bacon and Eggs

A dish to change the pace on Christmas morning and one which can be prepared on Christmas Eve, left in the fridge overnight and cooked in the morning while the presents are being opened.

10 slices white bread
55 g (2 oz) butter
10 slices lightly cooked bacon or ham
10 thin slices cheese
1 onion, finely chopped or grated
Half red/half green pepper, very finely diced
4 well-beaten eggs
570 ml (1 pint) milk or half milk/half cream
Few drops Tabasco sauce
Few drops Worcestershire sauce
¼ teasp. dried mustard
Salt and pepper

Butter the bread and arrange half the slices in a lightly oiled ovenproof dish. Layer on top slices of cooked ham and cheese alternately. Sprinkle with onion and finely diced peppers. I like to soften these vegetables by cooking in a little oil for 1-2 minutes. Cover with the remaining 5 slices of buttered bread.

In a separate bowl whisk the eggs, add the milk, Tabasco, Worcestershire sauce, dried mustard and seasoning. Then pour this mixture over the bread and leave to infuse for at least half an hour or preferably overnight. Bake in the oven at 190 °C (375 °F or regulo 5) for 25-30 minutes until cooked and golden-brown.

Serves 6-8

5   *From the Vegetable Patch*

egardless of the season, the shelves in our supermarkets and green-grocers now boast a wide variety of excellent vegetables, many of them home-grown. However, I feel there is nothing to beat the flavour of those vegetables we plant in the plot at the back of the house to pick and use on demand.

Cooking vegetables is all about bringing out the best of the flavours. I find a steamer one of the most useful utensils to get the best from any vegetable. My own steamer never gets time to cool down.

Many of my own favourite recipes are in this section and I have come up with ideas which are good to serve at family meal time as well as many simple ideas, ideal to serve at the 'Dinner' table with the least possible fuss. It's the treatment I have given them which makes the difference. The cooking times are generally short in order to serve the vegetables tender but with a little firmness.

Parsnip tarts—for those who don't like parsnips—are particularly good, this treatment giving them texture as well as bringing out their gentle sweetness.

Glazed fennel goes particularly well with fish and with gentle cooking the flavour becomes milder. Lemon and olive oil combine well with it. Caramelised sliced potatoes are so good that while writing this book I sat down with the photographers and ate the entire dish, but only after they had taken the photograph! It is important to cook the potatoes long enough until they become lightly golden-brown.

Country cabbage is a dish cooked in many homes as a good substantial vegetable, but if sprinkled with garlicky breadcrumbs, it changes its appeal entirely.

I only see Jerusalem artichokes around Christmas time so I always enjoy a dish of them cooked with a light cheesy sauce. They have a faint nutty flavour which can be enhanced with a sprinkling of nutmeg.

Pumpkin is another seasonal vegetable, one rarely used as a vegetable dish but if cooked with orange juice and onion and gently simmered, the flavour intensifies and is delicious.

51

Serving portions vary between 6 and 8—depending on need or greed.

Oven-baked mushrooms look after themselves, as do the aubergines baked with peppers.

If you can eat vegetables when in season, fresh garden peas taste better in June and July. Keep the Brussels sprouts for December.

Caramelised Sliced Potatoes with Garlic and Chives

900 g (2 lb) potatoes with skins on, cut into thick slices
55 g (2 oz) butter
2 cloves garlic, crushed
1 dessertsp. honey
30 g (1 oz) brown sugar
Salt and pepper
4 dessertsp. chives, finely chopped

Steam the potatoes until almost tender. Drain and allow to cool slightly. In a heavy-based pan heat the butter, and when sizzling add the crushed garlic, honey, brown sugar and seasoning. Mix together, then add the sliced potatoes. Toss the potatoes around until the sauce almost begins to caramelise and evaporate. Add the finely chopped chives and serve hot.

Oven-baked Layered Potatoes

This is one of my favourite ways to serve potatoes. This dish looks after itself in the oven and requires no split-second timing.

900 g (2 lb) potatoes, peeled and thinly sliced
3 spring onions, very finely chopped
Salt, pepper and nutmeg
2 eggs, lightly beaten
280 ml (½ pint) whipping cream
4 cloves garlic, finely chopped
140 g (5 oz) grated cheese, cheddar or Gruyère
55 g (2 oz) butter

Slice the potatoes and spring onions. Mix together in a bowl with the seasoning, nutmeg, lightly beaten eggs, whipping cream, garlic and half the cheese. Pour into a well-greased ovenproof dish, arranging the potatoes in layers. Dot with butter, sprinkle with remaining grated cheese and bake at 180 °C (350 °F or regulo 4) for approximately 1 hour. Place a little greased foil over the dish for the first half hour of cooking. Then remove to allow the top to become golden-brown.

Golden Potato Puffs

This is a very light way to serve potatoes and you can tuck a surprise filling of your choice, such as chopped chicken or diced vegetables, in the base of the potato shell before returning the soufflé mixture. Alternatively, the potatoes can be baked in an ovenproof dish after mixing with the other ingredients. They will cook and serve equally well.

4 medium potatoes for baking
280 ml (½ pint) milk
115 g (4 oz) grated cheddar cheese or Gruyère
Salt, pepper, pinch of paprika
½ onion, finely chopped
3 eggs, separated (reserve a little for brushing)
Sesame seeds or chopped parsley to serve

Heat the oven to 220 °C (425 °F or regulo 7). Scrub the potatoes, prick with a skewer, then bake in a pre-heated oven for approximately 1 hour (depending on size) until tender but still firm. Remove from the oven and slice in half lengthways. Scoop the soft flesh into a bowl and arrange the potato shells on a baking tray. In a saucepan heat the milk, add the cheese and seasoning, then stir in the cooked potato and onion. Cool slightly, then add the beaten egg yolks. Finally, fold in the stiffly beaten egg whites and return the mixture to the scooped-out potato shells, piling high. Or, if you wish to discard the shells, place the potato mixture in heaped tablespoons on a well-greased baking sheet. Brush with beaten egg, sprinkle with sesame seeds and bake in a hot oven at 200 °C (400 °F or regulo 6) for approximately 10 minutes until golden-brown and puffed up.

Crusty Baked Vegetables

This is another of my favourite vegetable dishes and one I like to serve if entertaining as it can be prepared ahead of time and is ideal for freezing.

1 medium aubergine
½ teasp. salt
1 onion
3 cloves garlic, crushed
1 red pepper
1 green pepper
2 courgettes
4 fresh tomatoes, diced
Salt and black pepper
½ teasp. oregano
280 ml (½ pint) vegetable stock
3 dessertsp. olive oil

Topping
55 g (2 oz) breadcrumbs (white or brown)
55 g (2 oz) grated cheddar cheese
30 g (1 oz) Parmesan cheese

Dice the vegetables into small pieces. Place the aubergine in a colander and sprinkle with half a teaspoon of salt to drain out the moisture. Leave for 30 minutes. Heat the oil in a pan, add the onions, garlic, peppers, courgettes and aubergine and cook over a low heat for 15-20 minutes. Add the diced tomatoes, seasoning, herbs and stock and allow to cook until softened, about 10 minutes. Pour into an ovenproof dish. Prepare the crumble topping by mixing the cheese and breadcrumbs together. Sprinkle over the vegetables and bake uncovered at 180 °C (350 °F or regulo 4) for half an hour until bubbling and crusty.

Country Cabbage

I like to use Savoy cabbage for this recipe as it combines the colours of the dark green and pale yellow leaves and looks exceptionally well.

1 Savoy cabbage, coarsely shredded

1 small onion, finely chopped
225 g (8 oz) streaky bacon, finely chopped
30 g (1 oz) melted butter
Salt and pepper

Steam the cabbage for 3-4 minutes. In a shallow frying pan, melt the fat and lightly fry the onion and finely chopped bacon for 2-3 minutes. Add the coarsely shredded cabbage and fry, tossing well until the cabbage has been well coated. Serve hot with garlicky breadcrumbs sprinkled on top, salt and freshly milled black pepper.

Roasted Vegetables with Garlic and Honey

This is a lovely, uncomplicated way to serve vegetables.

2 carrots
2 parsnips
450 g (1 lb) small baby potatoes
½ turnip
1 leek
2 dessertsp. olive oil
2 dessertsp. honey
3 cloves garlic, crushed
1 dessertsp. lemon juice
Salt and pepper

Cut the vegetables into good-sized pieces after washing really well. Plunge into a pan of boiling salted water for no longer than 1 minute. Drain, then place in a roasting tin with the warmed oil, honey and garlic. Toss the vegetables in the oil to coat well. The addition of 1 dessertsp. of lemon juice will help to improve the colour of the vegetables during roasting. Season, then roast in the oven at 180 °C (350 °F or regulo 4) for about 1 hour until golden-brown and tender.

Parsnip Tarts

For those who don't like parsnips!

4-5 parsnips
55 g (2 oz) butter
2 tablesp. milk
55 g (2 oz) plain flour
Pinch of mace
Salt and pepper
1 dessertsp. cooking oil

Wash, peel and dice the parsnips, then cook in a saucepan of boiling water, sufficient to cover the parsnips, until tender, 20-25 minutes. Mash very finely or whizz in a food processor until very smooth. When still warm, add the butter, seasoning, milk and flour. Mix well together, shape into little round uneven tarts and brown slowly in the oil for 2-3 minutes on either side. Drain on kitchen paper and serve hot.

Ribboned Carrots

This is such a quick way of cooking carrots. The main crop carrots are much richer in flavour than the little finger carrots of early summer. This dish reheats well.

3-4 large carrots
Knob of butter, melted
Pinch of sugar
3 tablesp. honey
Small piece root ginger, crushed
Black pepper

Peel the carrots thinly with a vegetable peeler, then shave off ribbons of carrots with the peeler, trying to get the length of the carrot in one sweep. You want to be able to use all the carrot, especially the central woody bit.

Steam the carrots for just a few minutes, then drain. Toss in a large pan to which the melted butter, sugar, honey and ginger have been added. Stir around to coat the carrots and serve with or without a little freshly milled black pepper.

Spring Vegetables in Disguise

6 florets each cauliflower and broccoli, and 6 each spring onions, small young carrots and new potatoes, all roughly chopped
55 g (2 oz) fresh garden peas
55 g (2 oz) grated cheese to finish

Creamy Buttery Sauce
30 g (1 oz) flour
55 g (2 oz) butter
Salt and pepper
140 ml (¼ pint) vegetable stock
½ teasp. grainy mustard
140 ml (¼ pint) cream

Cook each vegetable by steaming until cooked but still firm. The spring onions may not require cooking. Arrange the vegetables in a greased oven-proof dish.

Make the sauce by melting the fat in a saucepan. Gently blend in the flour and seasoning, add the mustard, cooled vegetable stock and finally the cream. Return to the heat and bring to boiling point, stirring well. Cook for 1 minute then pour the sauce over the vegetables.

Sprinkle the cheese over the sauce and either brown under the grill or in a moderate oven until bubbling.

Aromatic Pumpkin

This is a colourful and tasty vegetable dish but I feel pumpkin needs that little extra something during cooking to bring out its flavour.

900 g (2 lb) pumpkin, cut into chunks
1 large onion, finely chopped
2 tablesp. olive oil
1 orange, rind and juice
1 dessertsp. tomato purée
Salt and black pepper
½ teasp. paprika
1 dessertsp. finely shredded orange peel
1 dessertsp. finely chopped parsley or thyme to serve

Heat the oil in a pan, add the onion and cook gently over a low heat for approximately 5 minutes. In a separate pan, steam the pumpkin chunks for 10 minutes, then drain. To the onion add the pumpkin pieces, orange juice and rind, tomato purée and seasoning and cook for a further 5-6 minutes.

Serve sprinkled with finely shredded orange peel and chopped parsley or thyme.

Creamy Oven-baked Mushrooms

450 g (1 lb) fresh button mushrooms, sliced
1 small onion, finely chopped
2 tablesp. butter
2 tablesp. plain flour
140 ml (¼ pint) vegetable stock
140 ml (¼ pint) cream
2 tablesp. dry sherry
Salt and pepper
4 dessertsp. chopped parsley

Into a greased ovenproof dish place the sliced mushrooms and onion and dot with butter. Cover with foil and bake in the oven at 190 °C (375 °F or regulo 5) for 15 minutes. This is a great way to develop the flavour of the mushrooms.

In a bowl blend the flour with the cooled vegetable stock, cream and sherry. Add the seasoning and pour over the baking mushrooms, cover and return to the oven and cook for a further 15-20 minutes.

Serve hot, sprinkled liberally with freshly chopped parsley.

Oven-baked Peppers and Aubergines

The flavour of peppers becomes sweeter and very tasty if baked in this way. I like to combine them with strips of aubergines for a very colourful dish.

1 red pepper
1 green pepper } **cut into**
1 yellow pepper } **strips**
1 aubergine

2 dessertsp. olive oil
Black pepper
140 ml (¼ pint) vegetable stock
3-4 leaves fresh basil to serve

Cut the vegetables into coarse strips, trying to keep them the same size. Gently toss in hot olive oil in a pan. The aubergine will quickly absorb the oil so I find it better to add the peppers first. Transfer to an ovenproof dish, sprinkle with black pepper. Pour the vegetable stock over them and cover with foil. Bake in a pre-heated hot oven at 200 °C (400 °F or regulo 6) for 10-15 minutes until tender.

Serve with freshly chopped basil leaves if in season.

Grilled Peppers with Bacon

1 red pepper
1 green pepper
4 tomatoes, cut into quarters
225 g (8 oz) bacon, grilled and chopped
Seasoning
Fresh or dried basil
Olive oil to sprinkle on top

Wipe and cut the peppers in half lengthways, removing the seeds but leaving the stalks. Inside each half, place a tomato cut into quarters. Sprinkle with cooked chopped bacon, seasoning, herbs and olive oil. Place on the grill either on their own or in foil and cook until golden-brown and softened.

Garlicky Mushrooms

Serve these mushrooms in individual foil packets with a little butter in each one.

4 large flat mushrooms
115 g (4 oz) fine white breadcrumbs
1 dessertsp. cooking oil
4 cloves garlic, finely crushed
1 teasp. finely chopped parsley

Cook the crumbs in hot oil for 2-3 minutes, add the finely crushed garlic to the crumbs and continue cooking until well cooked. Allow the mixture to cool slightly before spooning on top of the mushrooms, flat side up. It is important to brush the mushrooms well with melted fat or oil to prevent them from drying up during cooking. Place each stuffed mushroom in its own foil packet, dot with butter and seal. Cook on the barbecue for 4-5 minutes or bake in the oven at 190 °C (375 °F or regulo 5) for 8-10 minutes. Serve garnished with the chopped parsley.

Honey and Lemon-glazed Fennel

Fennel is one of my favourite vegetables to serve with fish and when cooked, the flavour is mild.

2 heads fennel
30 g (1 oz) butter
4 dessertsp. runny honey
1 dessertsp. oil
1 dessertsp. demerara sugar
2 dessertsp. lemon juice

Prepare the fennel by removing the feathery tips. Cut the base off, then cut the bulbs into fine ribbon matchstick strips.

In a saucepan melt the butter, add the honey, oil and demerara sugar and fennel. Cook until the fennel shows signs of softening. I like to cook this vegetable until it shows signs of caramelising. When this stage is reached, add the lemon juice and cook until the liquid is absorbed. Cooking should take approximately 10 minutes; otherwise the flavour of the fennel is intense. Serve hot, garnished with a little knob of butter.

Spiced Gingered Beetroot

450 g (1 lb) fresh beetroot
30 g (1 oz) butter
1 tablesp. root ginger, grated
3 pineapple slices, diced
3 tablesp. white wine vinegar
2 tablesp. sugar

Salt and pepper
Chopped nuts to garnish

Cook the whole beetroot (including stalks) in boiling salted water for 1-2 hours. The skin will run off easily when cooked. Drain well, peel and cut into dice 0.5 cm (½ in.). Melt the butter in a saucepan, add the pineapple, vinegar, sugar, ginger and seasoning. Heat well, then pour over the beetroot. Serve sprinkled with chopped nuts.

Jerusalem Artichokes in a Cheesy Sauce

This lumpy vegetable has a most distinctive flavour. When choosing, pick out the smoothest, most evenly-sized ones; the knobblier they are, the more waste you will have. To obtain the required quantity of sliced artichokes, double the quantity by weight to start off with.

400 g (14 oz) trimmed weight of Jerusalem artichokes

Sauce
30 g (1 oz) melted fat
30 g (1 oz) plain flour
570 ml (1 pint) milk
200 g (7 oz) grated cheese, cheddar or Gruyère
Pinch of salt, black pepper and nutmeg

This white sauce made by the all-in-one method is very simple. Place the fat, flour and milk in a saucepan and mix well, gradually bringing up to boiling point. The cheese may be added at the beginning, although I find it easier to check the consistency by adding it at the end. Cook for a further minute to allow the cheese to melt. Add the seasoning.

Lay the sliced artichokes in a buttered dish, overlapping. Spoon the sauce over the slices, building up several layers. It is important to work quickly as the slices tend to discolour easily, although a light sprinkling of lemon juice helps to prevent this.

Bake at 180 °C (350 °F or regulo 4) for approximately 1 hour. The artichokes absorb much of the liquid and are ready when tender and golden on top. This makes a most interesting vegetable dish, ideal to serve with any meat.

6   *Saucy Ideas*

Today the variety of sauces is considerable, yet there is a swing towards lighter and more uncomplicated ones, with the option of using ingredients to suit the health conscious. In many recipes in this section, low-fat ingredients can be substituted for butter and cream with equally successful results.

My favourites are those which require the minimum of fuss yet retain their special something. Remember, it was Chaucer who said 'Woe to the cook whose sauce has no sting'.

All these sauce recipes are quick and easy to prepare with the emphasis on the unusual—rhubarb and redcurrant to serve with pan-fried duck and a highly-spirited sauce to serve with Slemish lamb, a colourful and tasty sauce which really brings out the best of the lamb.

The cold seafood sauce is ideal in that it can be made in advance and stored in a screw top jar in the fridge for up to 1 week. Syrupy maple sauce is delicious with hot baked puddings, especially if they have a hint of apple.

The foaming orange sabayon sauce has to be one of the most delicious sweet sauces I have ever tasted. The secret of this sauce, as with many another, is not to overcook, stir well and add the ingredients slowly. Most important, remember to taste before serving.

Hot Pink and Green Seafood Sauce

115 g (4 oz) cooked, shelled prawns
55 g (2 oz) butter
45 g (1½ oz) plain flour
280 ml (½ pint) fish stock or fish stock cube dissolved in
**   half pint boiling water**
140 ml (¼ pint) dry white wine

2 teasp. tomato purée or paste
2 tablesp. cream, lightly whipped
2 tablesp. cucumber, very finely chopped
Grinding of pink and green peppercorns
1 teasp. chopped dill or parsley

Melt the butter in a pan, add the flour and stir well over gentle heat for 1 minute. Remove from the heat and gradually stir in the stock and wine. Return to the heat and stir until the mixture boils and thickens. Next add the tomato purée, cream, prawns, cucumber and peppercorns and finally the dill. Heat without boiling and serve as soon as possible, as stirring spoils the colour of the dill.

Seafood Sauce (Cold)

140 ml (¼ pint) mayonnaise
2 dessertsp. lightly whipped cream or yoghurt
1 teasp. tomato purée
Few drops Tabasco sauce
Pinch of paprika
¼ cucumber, finely diced
1 dessertsp. finely chopped herbs, dill or parsley
Salt and pepper
55 g (2 oz) prawns (optional)

Mix all the ingredients together in a bowl. If liked, prawns can be added to enhance the texture of this sauce. Lovely served with cold salmon.

Sharp Lemon and Chive Butter

115 g (4 oz) butter, softened
Juice and rind of 1 lemon
2 dessertsp. chopped chives

In a bowl mix the softened butter with the chopped chives, lemon rind and juice. Mix well, then shape into little round pats and serve chilled from the fridge. Ideal with fish dishes.

Barbecue Sauce

1 onion, finely sliced
1 clove garlic, crushed
1 tablesp. oil
2 dessertsp. cider vinegar
1 teasp. grainy mustard
2 tablesp. soft brown sugar
Few drops of Worcestershire sauce
Pinch of salt and pepper
1 large tin tomatoes (400 g/14 oz)
1 dessertsp. tomato purée
170 g (6 oz) cooked vegetables (peppers, mushrooms,
    spring onions), lightly tossed in hot oil

Toss the crushed garlic and onion in hot oil for 1-2 minutes. Add the cider vinegar, grainy mustard, brown sugar, Worcestershire sauce and seasoning, cooking for a further 1-2 minutes until the sauce almost caramelises. Add the tin of tomatoes and 1 dessertsp. of tomato purée. Continue to cook for a further 3-4 minutes. After cooking, this sauce can be cooled and stored in a screw top jar in the fridge for up to 1 week.

For a more colourful sauce, add the lightly cooked sliced vegetables such as peppers, onions, and mushrooms. Heat through and serve hot.

Barbary Duck Breasts
with Rhubarb and Redcurrant Sauce

This rhubarb and redcurrant sauce is tangy, sharp and very colourful with pan-cooked duck breasts.

2 Barbary duck breasts (each approx. 115-170 g/4-6 oz)
1 dessertsp. oil
Black pepper and pinch of salt

Sauce
2 stalks rosy rhubarb
1 dessertsp. demerara sugar
115 g (4 oz) redcurrants
1 dessertsp. redcurrant jelly
140 ml (¼ pint) water

Heat the oil in a pan and add the seasoned duck breasts. Before adding, ensure the oil is hot enough to seal in the juices and to give a golden crisp to the outer coating of the duck. Cook approximately 3-4 minutes on either side, then cut into fine slices and serve with its accompanying sauce.

To prepare the sauce, gently poach the rhubarb in water and demerara sugar for 1-2 minutes before adding the redcurrants and jelly. Continue cooking until the fruits are well mixed and serve hot with lightly steamed potatoes, asparagus and baby carrots.

Slemish Lamb with a High-spirited Sauce

2 x 680 g (1½ lb) (approx.) racks of lamb
Oil for brushing

Marinade
2 tablesp. olive oil
2 tablesp. honey
2 tablesp. whiskey
A few sprigs of thyme and mint

Stuffing
1 onion, very finely chopped
55 g (2 oz) white breadcrumbs
2 teasp. mint, chopped
2 teasp. parsley, chopped
1 small parsnip, very finely diced
115 g (4 oz) apricots, finely chopped
1 lemon with rind, finely grated
1 egg, lightly whisked
Little salt and pepper

Sauce
70 ml (⅛ pint) lamb juices reduced from 140 ml (¼ pint)
2 dessertsp. honey
2 dessertsp. redcurrant jelly
70 ml (⅛ pint) whiskey
2-3 spring onions, finely chopped

Marinate the racks of lamb for 12-24 hours by mixing all the marinade ingredients together and spooning over the lamb at intervals.

Put all the ingredients for the stuffing in a bowl and bind them together using the lightly beaten egg. The secret of this stuffing lies in the fineness of the chopped ingredients. Stand the two racks of lamb together, concave sides facing, and carefully pack the stuffing into the cavity. Tie securely with string with the racks intertwined.

Place on foil on a meat roasting dish, lightly brush with oil, pour over the remainder of the marinade and roast in the oven at 200 °C (400 °F or regulo 6) for approximately 1 hour, depending on how rare you like to serve your lamb. A little longer cooking may be necessary. To prevent the bones from browning during cooking, I find it a good idea to wrap a little foil around them.

To make this wonderfully tasty high-spirited sauce, drain the meat juices from around the lamb just before serving and reduce to about 70 ml (⅛ pint). Next add the honey, redcurrant jelly and bring to boiling point. Finally add the whiskey and the finely chopped spring onion. Turn off the heat immediately and serve.

Remember to remove the string from the lamb before serving.

I like to serve the Slemish Lamb with lightly steamed, assorted seasonal vegetables served around the lamb on a large platter.

Serves 6-8

Peppered Mushroom Sauce

A lovely sauce to serve with steaks. The brandy is optional but it helps to sharpen the sauce.

225 g (8 oz) button mushrooms
½ onion, very finely chopped
30 g (1 oz) butter
45 g (1½ oz) plain flour
280 ml (½ pint) chicken stock
140 ml (¼ pint) cream
½ teasp. freshly ground black pepper
1-2 tablesp. brandy (optional)

Melt the butter and when hot add the onion and mushrooms, cooking for 1-2 minutes. Remove from the heat and add the flour, mixing well with the cold stock and cream. Cook until the sauce shows signs of bubbling and thickening. Add the pepper and brandy, cook for 1 minute and serve hot.

Bread Sauce

280 ml (½ pint) milk
1 onion, studded with 10 cloves
1 bay leaf
Pinch of dried mace
30 g (1 oz) butter
55 g (2 oz) fine white breadcrumbs
Pinch of salt

Heat the milk in a saucepan. Add the studded onion and leave to infuse for 10 minutes. Strain, then to the flavoured milk add the bay leaf, mace, butter, breadcrumbs and seasoning. Cook gently for 5 minutes, then serve in a sauce boat. Remove the bay leaf before serving.

This sauce is particularly good with roast chicken, turkey or pheasant.

Hot Peppery Sauce

This sauce will enliven any dish of pork, chicken or lamb and is also very colourful.

3 peppers (1 red, 1 green, 1 yellow), finely diced
2 onions, finely diced
3 cloves garlic, crushed
1 dessertsp. oil
1 teasp. mustard
½ teasp. turmeric powder
½ teasp. grated root ginger
1 tablesp. soft brown sugar
1 tablesp. tomato purée
2 tablesp. cider vinegar
140 ml (¼ pint) vegetable stock

Heat the oil in a pan and lightly cook the finely diced peppers, onion and garlic for 2-3 minutes. Add the remaining ingredients, bring to the boil and simmer for 5 minutes. Serve hot.

Be careful not to overcook this sauce or the colours of the vegetables will spoil.

Fluffy Lemon Sauce

A good tangy lemon sauce is ideal to sharpen the flavour of many a simple pudding. This sauce also has an interesting texture.

2 eggs, beaten
30 g (1 oz) caster sugar
Juice of 2 lemons
Rind of 1 lemon
70 ml (⅛ pint) white wine, preferably dry

In a bowl beat the eggs and sugar until light and fluffy. Add the lemon juice and rind and the white wine. Place the bowl over a pan of hot water and beat until the sauce thickens. Be careful not to overheat. This sauce makes a tangy change to serve with Christmas pudding.

Foaming Orange Sabayon Sauce

This is a rich foaming sauce and one of the most delicious I have tasted. My favourite way to serve it is while still warm over ice cream or a fruit pie, but it is delicious on its own served in pretty glasses dusted with chocolate and cinnamon powder. This sauce can be lightly flavoured with sherry, Marsala, Grand Marnier or a sweet white wine.

4 large egg yolks
4 level tablesp. caster sugar
Juice of 1 orange
2 level teasp. cornflour or arrowroot
3 tablesp. Marsala, wine or Grand Marnier

In a bowl beat the egg yolks and sugar together until light and fluffy. This is one of the most important stages in the making of this sauce; if not sufficiently well beaten, the sauce will be thin. Add the orange juice, blended with the cornflour or arrowroot, the Marsala, wine or Grand Marnier and mix well. Place the bowl over a saucepan of hot water and continue whisking until the sauce becomes frothy. Be careful that the water in the pan does not boil rapidly or the sauce will curdle. Whisk continually for about 8 minutes until the sauce is frothy and lightly cooked. This sauce should hold for up to half an hour if kept in a warm place.

Syrupy Maple Sauce

A delicious sweet sauce to serve with apple pie or baked apples.

55 g (2 oz) butter
2 dessertsp. honey
140 ml (¼ pint) maple syrup
Pinch of nutmeg
140 ml (¼ pint) whipping cream or double cream
15 g (½ oz) blended cornflour (if required)

Melt the butter in a saucepan, add honey, maple syrup, and nutmeg, stirring all the time. Next add the lightly whipped cream or double cream and heat but do not allow to boil. Overheating will thin the sauce.

If you feel the sauce is a little on the thin side, it can be thickened by the addition of 15 g (½ oz) blended cornflour.

Rich Dark Chocolate Sauce

225 g (8 oz) soft, dark brown sugar
85 g (3 oz) butter
3 tablesp. cocoa powder
1 teasp. vanilla essence or extract
2 tablesp. golden syrup
1 tablesp. runny honey
280 ml (½ pint) boiling water
2 dessertsp. whipping cream

Into a saucepan place the sugar, butter, cocoa powder, vanilla, syrup and honey and mix well over a very gentle heat. Add the boiling water and bring up to boiling point, stirring all the time. Allow to cool slightly before adding the whipping cream. Mix well and serve.

Makes approximately 280 ml (½ pint).

Rhubarb and Rosehip Syrup

Here is a very tasty syrup which will transform a rice pudding or add that special flavour to vanilla ice cream. It is an interesting way to liven up frozen rhubarb.

115 g (4 oz) rosehips
280 ml (½ pint) water
2-3 stalks rhubarb and 1 dessertsp. water
115 g (4 oz) granulated sugar

Prepare the rosehip syrup by removing the stalks from the rosehips, then poach in a saucepan with the water and sugar until soft and syrupy. Strain through a very fine sieve.

In a separate pan gently poach the rhubarb in 1 dessertsp. of water. If the rhubarb has been frozen, you may not need to add water during poaching. When soft, mix with the rosehip syrup and heat gently. Serve hot or cold. Rosehip cordial can now be bought in many supermarkets as a speedy alternative to making your own.

Good Family Mulled Apple Sauce

3 apples, peeled, cored and diced
55 g (2 oz) demerara sugar
140 ml (¼ pint) each of water and apple juice, mixed
15 g (½ oz) butter, softened
1 dessertsp. cider vinegar
2 cloves
1 stick cinnamon

Place the apples, sugar, water, apple juice, butter and cider vinegar in a saucepan. Add the cinnamon stick and cloves—these can be tied in a muslin bag as they are easier to remove after cooking. Cover and simmer over low heat until the apples become soft and mushy approximately 10-15 minutes. Serve warm with your favourite steamed pudding.

7 *Grand Finales*

Many of my pudding recipes have been passed from family to family and friend to friend, each gaining a little interest on the way. These puddings are part of a cook's heritage and have special appeal. There is something very comforting about warm puddings and their sauces, but I have also included a selection of cold puddings which will take you through the summer and well into the winter. I once read somewhere 'No mean woman can cook well' and this epitomises my feelings when it comes to puddings.

Bread and butter pudding is having a revival, appearing now on hotel menus, each one varying in quantities of cream, fruit and type of bread used. This recipe develops a lovely eggy custard base with a light bread topping. The success of this pudding lies in the careful balance of not too much bread to custard.

Harvest time pudding is a much better behaved version of that most tricky summer pudding where the bread is expected to stand to attention. I feel it's asking quite a lot so I prefer this sleepier version with the bread lined across the top. Try vanilla sauce for a pleasant change from custard. If you can find vanilla extract or vanilla pod in your local store, the flavour will be much better.

Passion fruit transforms the flavour of a good rice pudding—one of my favourites. Just spread on top before covering with an orange-flavoured meringue. If you like a pudding that is neither hot nor cold, then summer fruits in an Irish mist is just the one. This pudding combines chilled fresh fruit with a warm grilled sauce, dusted with icing sugar.

For a real indulgence try hot chocolate pots, a rich dark soufflé which is also delicious served with vanilla sauce. Some of my favourite cold puddings which take very little time to prepare are rum-baked bananas, winter strawberries and elderflower syllabub.

Harvest Time Pudding with Vanilla Sauce

450 g (1 lb) mixed fruits (apples, blackberries, plums)
140 ml (¼ pint) concentrated apple juice
1 teasp. cinnamon
55 g (2 oz) demerara sugar
7-8 slices day-old bread, cut into triangles
1 egg, beaten

In a saucepan, gently poach the fruits in the apple juice, cinnamon and demerara sugar until just showing signs of softening. Pour into a serving dish, arrange the slices of bread over the top of the fruit, brush with lightly beaten egg and sprinkle with some demerara sugar. Leave the bread to infuse in the fruit juices for at least 5 minutes before baking in the oven at 190 °C (375 °F or regulo 5) for 15-20 minutes or until the bread becomes crispy and golden-brown. Serve with vanilla sauce.

Serves 4

Vanilla Sauce
1 vanilla pod or few drops vanilla extract
30 g (1 oz) caster sugar
4 egg yolks, beaten
570 ml (1 pint) milk

Place the vanilla pod in a bowl with the sugar and leave the flavour to impart (at least half an hour). As an alternative to vanilla pod, a few drops of vanilla extract can be added to the sugar and left to infuse for the same length of time. Beat the eggs and sugar until smooth and creamy. Warm the milk in a saucepan and pour over the egg mixture. Mix well, then return to the saucepan and over a very gentle heat, stir until the sauce is thick enough to coat the back of a spoon. It is important to keep the temperature low during the making of this sauce; otherwise it will curdle. Serve warm.

Passionate Rice Pudding with Orange Meringue

225 g (8 oz) pudding rice
850 ml (1½ pints) milk
30 g (1 oz) caster sugar
3 passion fruits

Meringue
2 egg whites
115 g (4 oz) caster sugar
Rind of 1 orange
1 dessertsp. orange juice

Topping
30 g (1 oz) demerara sugar

Place the rice, sugar and milk in a greased ovenproof dish. Bake in the oven at 180 °C (350 °F or regulo 4) for approximately 1 hour until the rice absorbs the milk and becomes soft and creamy. Stir the rice at intervals during cooking—this should help the creamy texture. Remove from the oven and scoop the centre of the passion fruits over the rice, spreading evenly over the top.

Make the meringue by whisking the egg whites until stiff. Gently fold in the caster sugar, 1 dessertsp. at a time. Finally add the grated orange rind and 1 dessertsp. of orange juice. Pile the meringue high on top of the pudding. Sprinkle with demerara sugar and bake at 180 °C (350 °F or regulo 4) for approximately 10 minutes until the meringue is golden and crisp.

Serves 6

Bread and Butter Pudding

This is a much more glamorous version of the pudding I remember as a child. It has a rich eggy custard and plumped up sultanas with a lovely crusty top. Serve with yoghurt or lightly whipped cream.

4 slices of white bread
30 g (1 oz) butter
115 g (4 oz) sultanas
½ teasp. cinnamon
4 dessertsp. apple or fruit juice
570 ml (1 pint) milk or half milk/half cream
55 g (2 oz) caster sugar
½ teasp. vanilla essence
4 egg yolks, whisked
30 g (1 oz) demerara sugar
30 g (1 oz) sultanas

In a bowl mix together the sultanas, cinnamon and apple juice. Leave aside for at least half an hour to allow the sultanas to plump up, then place in an ovenproof dish. In a saucepan, heat the milk with the caster sugar, vanilla and whisked egg yolks. Do not allow to boil but stir until showing signs of thickening. Remove from heat.

Butter the slices of bread, cut into triangles and arrange them over the sultanas, overlapping. Pour the eggy custard over the sultana mixture and leave this pudding to sit for at least 15 minutes before baking, as the bread will absorb the liquid and cook much better. Sprinkle with 30 g (1 oz) demerara sugar and 30 g (1 oz) sultanas before baking at 190 °C (375 °F or regulo 5) for 20-25 minutes until crisp and golden-brown on top.

Serves 4

Summer Fruits in an Irish Mist

Any seasonal fruits can be used in this pudding. The flavour is best if they are fresh and it can be made using any combination. Try strawberries, kiwi fruits, peaches, oranges and grapes for a summer pudding, or for the autumn try blackberries, blueberries and apples.

450 g (1 lb) fresh fruits, peeled if necessary and sliced
3 large egg yolks
2 dessertsp. caster sugar
2-3 dessertsp. sweet white wine
2-3 dessertsp. Cointreau, Grand Marnier or Irish Mist
140 ml (¼ pint) cream
30 g (1 oz) icing sugar
Pinch of grated nutmeg

Prepare the fruits and place in a shallow serving dish. If wished, they can be sprinkled with a little sugar. In a bowl beat the egg yolks and caster sugar until fluffy, add the wine, liqueur and cream. Over a saucepan of hot water, beat the sauce until it thickens, approximately 10 minutes. Be careful that the water in the saucepan does not boil; otherwise the sauce will curdle. When the sauce thickens and becomes smooth, pour it over the fruit, dust with icing sugar and nutmeg and place under a hot grill until the sauce shows signs of browning. Serve warm.

Serves 6

Apricot and Almond Brulée

A simple, tasty pudding with the dried fruits initially cooked in fresh orange juice and cinnamon, which allows them to plump up and become full of flavour.

140 ml (¼ pint) orange juice, fresh
225 g (8 oz) dried apricots, sliced
2 tablesp. Grand Marnier (optional)
115 g (4 oz) muscatel raisins
115 g (4 oz) golden sultanas
2 pears, finely sliced
1 teasp. cinnamon powder
55 g (2 oz) flaked almonds
140 ml (¼ pint) fromage frais, cream or yoghurt
2 dessertsp. honey
55 g (2 oz) demerara sugar

In a saucepan, heat the orange juice and if wished, a little orange liqueur. Add the sliced apricots, raisins, sultanas, sliced pears and ½ teasp. cinnamon powder. Poach the fruit lightly in a covered pan for 2-3 minutes. Turn off the heat and leave to cool as the fruit absorbs all the liquid and plumps up. Transfer to a greased ovenproof dish and sprinkle with flaked almonds. In a separate bowl, mix the fromage frais or lightly whipped cream with honey and the remaining cinnamon. Pour over the fruit, sprinkle the top with demerara sugar and flash under the grill for 1-2 minutes until golden-brown.

Serves 6

Berry Brulée

I find the texture of Greek yoghurt best for this dish and you can vary the fruits as the seasons change. My favourite is made with blackberries and raspberries, with a few strawberries for extra flavour.

450 g (1 lb) assorted berries (raspberries, blackberries, strawberries)
140 ml (¼ pint) Greek yoghurt
Pinch of nutmeg
30 g (1 oz) caster sugar
55 g (2 oz) demerara sugar
1 tablesp. water

Wash the fruit and dry carefully. Gently crush the fruits together in a bowl. In a separate bowl, mix the yoghurt with 2 dessertsp. of the crushed fruit and add a pinch of nutmeg. Place the crushed fruit in a serving bowl and sprinkle with caster sugar. Pour the yoghurt and berry mixture over the fruit and smooth the top.

In a small saucepan, heat the demerara sugar with 1 tablesp. water, bring to the boil and bubble until it forms a dark golden caramel. Gently drizzle this over the yoghurt and flash under a hot grill for 30 seconds, then serve.

Serves 6

Hot Chocolate Pots

These soufflés cook better in individual ramekin dishes. Choose small ones as this pudding is rich, dark and delicious.

85 g (3 oz) caster sugar
45 g (1½ oz) plain flour
30 g (1 oz) butter
30 g (1 oz) cocoa powder
140 ml (¼ pint) milk
4 eggs, separated
30 g (1 oz) melted butter and caster sugar to prepare the
ramekins

Prepare the ramekin dishes by greasing with melted butter and dust with 1 dessertsp. of the caster sugar. In a separate bowl or blender, mix the remaining sugar, flour, cocoa and butter. This mixture may look a little crumbly. Heat the milk but do not allow to boil. Then add to the crumbly cocoa mixture and whisk. Add the separated whisked egg yolks slowly, mixing well during their addition. Finally add the whisked egg whites in stages. Mix well at the beginning, then fold gradually until all has been mixed. Divide between 5-6 ramekin dishes and bake at 200 °C (400 °F or regulo 6) for approximately 15 minutes until firm. These little hot soufflés will cook better in a bain marie; place them in a pan of warm water reaching half way up the ramekin dishes.

Serves 5-6

Steamed Jam Pudding

4 dessertsp. strawberry jam
115 g (4 oz) butter
115 g (4 oz) caster sugar
2 eggs, beaten
170 g (6 oz) self-raising cake flour
1 tablesp. milk, if needed
Vanilla or custard sauce to serve

Grease a 1.1 L (2 pint) pudding basin and spoon the strawberry jam into the bottom. Cream the butter and sugar until light and fluffy, add the eggs and flour alternately and if necessary 1 tablesp. of milk to mix to a soft dropping consistency. Pour this mixture into the pudding basin and cover with greaseproof paper. Tie securely, steam for 1 hour. (This pudding cooks extremely well in the microwave. Allow 6 minutes on full power and 2 minutes standing time.)

Serve hot. If allowed to cool and stand, the pudding cooked in the microwave can become quite firm. Serve with vanilla or custard sauce.

Serves 6

Christmas Pudding Ice Cream with Hot Mincemeat Sauce

This recipe can be varied easily with Christmas fruits. As time is precious in the weeks before Christmas this is a great pudding to make in advance and store in the freezer. Using your own favourite ice cream recipe, you can make your own version and add an assortment of fruits to it. However, as often happens, time disappears, so bought ice cream will do equally well and you can add your own special flavour to the fruits. The hot mincemeat sauce is especially good combined with cold ice cream.

Ice Cream

450 g (1 lb) vanilla ice cream
115 g (4 oz) cherries, fresh or tinned
55 g (2 oz) candied peel
55 g (2 oz) sultanas
4 tablesp. brandy
30 g (1 oz) pecan nuts or walnuts

In a large bowl soften the ice cream and add the chopped cherries, candied peel, sultanas, brandy and finely chopped nuts. Mix well together, then transfer to a 1.1 L (2 pint) pudding basin and press down well. Return to the freezer and store until required.

Hot Mincemeat Sauce
Rind and juice of 1 orange and 1 lemon
140 ml (¼ pint) water
225 g (8 oz) soft brown sugar
2 tablesp. rum
1 small Cox's apple, cored, peeled and diced
55 g (2 oz) currants
55 g (2 oz) raisins
55 g (2 oz) sultanas
½ teasp. mixed spice
½ teasp. cinnamon
1 teasp. arrowroot, blended with juice of ½ orange
30 g (1 oz) flaked almonds to serve

Place the orange and lemon rind in enough water to cover and boil for 2 minutes, then drain. In a separate pan, bring to the boil the water, brown sugar, rum, apple, currants, raisins, sultanas, spices and arrowroot blended with the juice of ½ orange. Bubble gently until the sauce resembles toffee and is a golden-brown colour. Add the orange and lemon rind. The flaked almonds can be added to this sauce before serving.

Serve the mincemeat sauce poured over the top of the ice cream.
Serves 6-8

Brandied Peaches

4 peaches
4 dessertsp. honey
30 g (1 oz) demerara sugar
2 dessertsp. brandy
140 ml (¼ pint) cream or yoghurt

Cut the peaches in half and place in foil parcels. Cover with honey and demerara sugar and heat under the grill until the fruit shows signs of softening. Spoon the brandy over the peaches during cooking. Serve hot with whipped cream or yoghurt.
Serves 4

Hot Grilled Marshmallows

10 marshmallows
10 strawberries
4 kebab sticks

Skewer the marshmallows and strawberries with the kebab sticks. Set on the hot barbecue for 1-2 minutes until the marshmallows show signs of softening and turn golden-brown. Serve warm.

Serves 4

Lemon and Rum-baked Bananas

4 bananas
4 dessertsp. lemon juice
2 dessertsp. honey
55 g (2 oz) demerara sugar
Sprinkling of dark rum
140 ml (¼ pint) whipped cream or yoghurt
  and 115 g (4 oz) flaked toasted almonds to serve

Split the bananas lengthways in their skins and place in a foil parcel. Sprinkle with lemon juice, honey, demerara sugar and a little rum. Leave to cook until the banana softens. Serve with whipped cream or yoghurt and flaked almonds.

Serves 4

Glazed Fruit Kebabs

Assorted fruits (banana, kiwi, strawberries, peaches,
  apricots and pears)
Sprinkling of lemon juice
2 dessertsp. liqueur or fruit juice
55 g (2 oz) demerara sugar

Arrange the pieces of fruit on kebab sticks. Sprinkle with lemon juice, liqueur or fruit juice, demerara sugar and grill for 1-2 minutes.

Serves 4

Blackberry Mist

450 g (1 lb) blackberries
30 g (1 oz) caster sugar

Egg Custard
570 ml (1 pint) milk
4 egg yolks
1 dessertsp. blended cornflour
30 g (1 oz) gelatine, dissolved in 1 dessertsp. warm water
115 ml (4 oz) whipped cream
115 ml (4 oz) yoghurt
2 egg whites, beaten

Wash the blackberries in cold water. Sprinkle with caster sugar and place half in the bottom of a serving bowl.

Make the egg custard by blending the milk, egg yolks and cornflour. Heat gently until the custard shows signs of thickening but do not allow it to boil.

Purée the remaining blackberries by passing through a sieve or if liked, just soften lightly with a fork. Add these blackberries to the egg custard, pour in the dissolved gelatine, mixing well. Next add the whipped cream and yoghurt. Finally add the beaten egg whites and pour over the blackberries in the serving dish.

Decorate with a sprig of blackberry after chilling in the fridge for about 1 hour.

Elderflower Syllabub

With elderflower cordial now widely available in many stores, the flavour of this summertime pudding can be enjoyed all year round. I prefer to make this pudding with fresh elderflowers as the flavour is more intense.

Syrup
6 elderflower heads, washed
115 ml (4 fl. oz) water
85 g (3 oz) caster sugar

280 ml (½ pint) double cream
2 tablesp. sweet white wine
1 egg white, whisked
Almond biscuits to serve

To prepare the syrup, heat the water in a saucepan, add the sugar and stir until dissolved. Add the washed elderflower heads and leave to infuse for at least 10 minutes. When cool, strain the syrup.

In a separate bowl, beat the cream very lightly; do not allow it to become thick. Add the wine, strained elderflower syrup and finally fold in the beaten egg white. Pour into individual glasses and chill before serving with almond biscuits.

Serves 3-4

Winter/Summer Strawberries

This delicious dessert is so easy to make in the middle of winter with strawberries which are now available in our supermarkets all year round.

450 g (1 lb) strawberries, hulls removed
30 g (1 oz) icing sugar or caster sugar
140 ml (¼ pint) whipped cream
140 ml (¼ pint) Greek yoghurt or fromage frais
170 g (6 oz) crushed almond macaroon or ratafia biscuits
2 dessertsp. kirsch (optional)
55 g (2 oz) toasted nuts to decorate
Sprigs of mint

Mix the strawberries with the sugar and crush lightly. Reserve a few whole berries to decorate at the end. In a separate bowl, whip the cream lightly and mix with the yoghurt. Fold in the lightly crushed biscuits and fruit and stir until a light marbling effect is achieved. A little extra sugar may be added, along with 2 dessertsp. kirsch to enhance the flavour. Serve in pretty glasses, sprinkled with toasted nuts a fresh berry and a sprig of mint. This pudding can also be made successfully with raspberries or blackberries.

Serves 6

Down Under Peach Melba

I like to serve this pudding in tall pretty glasses. The flavours epitomise the best of summer foods.

340 g (12 oz) fresh raspberries
30 g (1 oz) caster sugar
6 ripe peaches or nectarines
3 tablesp. icing sugar
1 dessertsp. sweet white wine
140 ml (¼ pint) cream, yoghurt or crème fraiche
30 g (1 oz) toasted hazelnuts and sprigs of mint to decorate

Sprinkle the raspberries with 30 g (1 oz) caster sugar. Peel the peaches or nectarines, then either mash very finely with a fork or blend in a food processor with the icing sugar until very smooth; add the white wine. Into tall glasses pour a little of the peach syrup, then raspberries, then a little more syrup on top of the raspberries and decorate with yoghurt, cream or crème fraiche.

Decorate with a sprig of mint and sprinkle with toasted nuts.
Serves 6

Macaroon Meringue

Meringue
3 egg whites
170 g (6 oz) soft brown sugar
85 g (3 oz) toasted almonds, finely chopped
Few drops vanilla essence
Few drops almond essence

Filling
570 ml (1 pint) whipped cream or cream and yoghurt mixed
115 g (4 oz) apricots, finely chopped

Topping
115 g (4 oz) almond macaroon biscuits, crushed
55 g (2 oz) toasted ground almonds
30 g (1 oz) soft brown sugar

4-5 apricots and 30 g (1 oz) toasted flaked almonds to decorate

Make the meringue in the usual way but use soft brown sugar. At the end, fold in the finely chopped toasted almonds and the essences. Transfer the meringue to 3 lined baking sheets with a rectangular shape drawn on each one, approximately 20 cm x 7.5 cm (8 in. x 3 in.). Spoon the meringue on to each shape and using a palette knife, flatten each meringue and bake in the oven at 120 °C (250 °F or regulo ½) for approximately 1 hour until firm.

When cooked and cool, spread each layer of meringue with whipped cream and finely chopped apricots. Build up the 3 layers of meringue, one on top of the other. Reserve some cream to cover the sides and top.

Mix together the finely crushed macaroon biscuits, toasted ground almonds and soft brown sugar. Spread evenly over the meringue tower along the top and sides. Decorate with finely chopped apricot and flaked almonds.

Serves 6

Fresh Berry Ice Cream

One of the quickest and tastiest ice cream recipes I have, this version can be made with your favourite berries or summer fruits.

**450 g (1 lb) fruit—a mixture of strawberries, raspberries,
blackberries
225 g (8 oz) icing sugar
280 ml (½ pint) double cream
140 ml (¼ pint) Greek yoghurt**

Wash, dry and hull the fruit, cut into small pieces, gently crush with a fork, then sprinkle with sieved, icing sugar. Cover and set aside for half an hour, then purée in a food processor. In a separate bowl, whip cream, add the vanilla, puréed fruit and yoghurt. Mix well, then transfer to a shallow container and place in the freezer. During the freezing process remove the ice cream from the freezer several times, tip into a bowl and beat gently to break up the ice crystals. Return to the freezer after beating and serve when firm.

Serves 6

8 *An Apple a Day*

The apple tree in our garden grew the best apples I have ever tasted, not the biggest and rosiest but the sweetest, and the flavour was so good. Just before they ripened, the winds came along with expected regularity and blew them from the tree. So necessity being the mother of invention, we set to picking and using them before the wasps and blackbirds descended on them.

There are few flavours and tastes to match the sweet subtle flavour and crunch of home-grown apples. I like to use eaters in many desserts as they are less tart and more aromatic. However they can be difficult to purée so a good whizz in a food processor may be needed. Apples combine very well with other seasonal ingredients such as nuts and blackberries. What could be tastier than home-made blackberry and apple pie wrapped in a sweet crumbly pastry or baked stuffed apples with honey and raisins? Apples also add a superior touch to many a vegetable dish such as braised hot pickled red cabbage.

To preserve the flavour of apples in liquid form, try apple cordial—not quite so potent as Joe-Grundy-from-the-Archers' home brew! Apart from drinking it, apple cordial can be put to good use when poaching apples and berries.

Remember, when buying apples, big does not always mean best and I find the medium-sized ones have a better flavour. As a rule three apples should weigh about a pound. If you can't keep up with the abundance of fruit in late autumn then remember that apples freeze extremely well for up to six months. Peel, core and slice them thickly, blanch in boiling water for just 1 minute. Drain, then plunge them into cold water and pack either in ridge containers or polythene bags dusted with a little sugar.

Don't forget the children. After all they love apples and the saying 'an apple a day keeps the doctor away' works just as effectively with toffee apples.

Apricot and almond brulée

Blackberry and apple pie

Apple picking

Baked Bramley apples with raisins and hazelnuts

Simnel cake

Hot cross Irish soda bread with herbs

Beekeeper's cake with nutmeg

Spiced wholemeal biscuits

Fresh fruit Pavlova

Rhubarb and lavender jelly

Home-made strawberry jam

Preserving autumn in Jenny's kitchen

Toffee Apples

My sister Rosie always made the toffee apples in our house. Although a good cook in her own right she does not share my love of cooking. She firmly believes that if she works hard and prospers well, someone else will do the cooking for her.

6-8 small red eating apples

Caramel
225 g (8 oz) granulated sugar
A little water, approx. 2-3 tablesp.
Pinch of cream of tartar

To make the caramel, put the sugar in a small saucepan and add sufficient water to moisten it, approximately 2-3 tablesp. Dissolve over a gentle heat and stir in the cream of tartar. Bring to the boil and simmer gently until golden-brown. Remove from the heat, allow the bubbles to subside and quickly dip the apples in the caramel. Cool on a greased surface.

The cream of tartar helps prevent the sugar from crystallising.

Sparkling Fruit Drink

A good non-alcoholic punch is always popular for those guests who may be driving or who may just prefer not to drink alcohol. This punch resembles the flavour of tangy home-made lemonade.

1 orange }
2 lemons } **juice of**
115 g (4 oz) caster sugar
1.1 L (2 pints) water
1.1 L (2 pints) apple juice
1.1 L (2 pints) ginger ale
Fresh strawberries, finely sliced
Sprigs of garden mint to serve
Crushed ice

Cut the orange and lemons in half and squeeze the juice into a large saucepan. Add the sugar and water and bring to the boil, stirring until the sugar has dissolved. For extra sharpness, the lemon and orange shells can be added to the syrup mixture and used until boiling point is reached.

Leave to cool, then strain into a punch or serving bowl. Chill really well. Then just before serving add the apple juice, ginger ale, crushed ice and strawberries, and mint to decorate.

Blackberry and Apple Pie

Sweet Pastry
285 g (10 oz) plain flour
200 g (7 oz) sunflower margarine or butter, softened
55 g (2 oz) caster sugar
1 egg yolk

Filling
450 g (1 lb) cooking apples, peeled, cored and thinly sliced
115 g (4 oz) blackberries
2 dessertsp. cider, apple juice or water
55 g (2 oz) demerara sugar
10 whole cloves
15 g (½ oz) cornflour (optional)

To brush pastry: 1 egg, beaten
Caster sugar to serve

To make the pastry, sieve the flour into a bowl, add the softened fat, cut and rub through. Add the caster sugar and egg yolk to mix to a soft dough. Cover the pastry with cling film and leave to relax and firm up in the fridge for at least half an hour.

To make the filling, put the apple juice, demerara sugar and cloves into a saucepan and heat. Add the apples and cook for 1-2 minutes, stirring to coat and soften the apples. Add the blackberries and leave to cool. If the berries are ripe and full of juice, then the addition of 15 g (½ oz) of blended cornflour to the fruit will help prevent the pastry becoming soggy during cooking.

Roll out two-thirds of the pastry and use to line an 20 cm (8 in.) pie dish. Brush the base of the pastry with beaten egg to seal it during cooking. Add the apples and blackberries, draining off some of the juices. Roll out the remaining third of the pastry into a circle 18 cm (7 in.) diameter, brush the pastry edges with beaten egg and place on the top. Seal the edges together. Brush top with the remaining beaten egg and bake at 190 °C (375 °F or regulo 5) for 20-25 minutes until golden-brown. Serve dusted with caster sugar.

If preferred, the pastry for the top of this pie can be cut into narrow strips and latticed across the top.

Baked Bramley Apples with Raisins and Hazelnuts

6 large apples
115 g (4 oz) sun-dried seedless raisins
30 g (1 oz) hazelnuts
115 g (4 oz) blackberries
225 g (8 oz) brown sugar
230 ml (8 fl. oz) water
Half a vanilla pod (or 2 drops vanilla essence)
115 ml (4 fl. oz) dark rum
6 teasp. butter
6 tablesp. brown sugar

Put the sugar and water in a heavy saucepan with the vanilla essence and cook over medium heat, stirring until the sugar has dissolved. Then simmer for 5 minutes. Remove from the heat and stir in the hazelnuts and raisins. Leave to cool, add the blackberries and remove the vanilla pod.

Core the apples, then put each one on a square of double thickness aluminium foil. Fill the centre of each apple with the rum-soaked raisins and blackberries, top each one with 1 teasp. of butter, then sprinkle over with 1 tablesp. of brown sugar.

These can either be baked in the oven or placed on foil and cooked on the barbecue over medium hot coals for 10-15 minutes or until the apples are soft but holding their shape. Serve hot with whipped cream.

Serves 6

Bramley and Roasted Nut Cake

This is a layered pudding which serves as a cake if allowed to cool.

Pastry
170 g (6 oz) plain flour
55 g (2 oz) soft brown sugar
Pinch of nutmeg
115 g (4 oz) fat
1 egg yolk
Add enough water to mix to a stiff dough

Filling
2 Bramley apples, sliced
85 g (3 oz) demerara sugar
2 dessertsp. cold water

Sponge mixture
115 g (4 oz) butter
115 g (4 oz) soft brown sugar
85 g (3 oz) self-raising cake flour
2 large eggs
55 g (2 oz) ground almonds
55 g (2 oz) almonds, flaked

Topping
85 g (3 oz) caster sugar
1 lemon (juice only)
1 dessertsp. honey
2 dessertsp. Calvados (apple brandy)

First make the pastry. Sieve the flour into a large bowl, add the soft brown sugar and nutmeg. Then cut through and rub the fat in roughly, add the egg yolk and sufficient water to mix to a stiff dough. This pastry may require very little water to mix if the fat is rubbed well into the flour. Roll out the pastry to line the base of a 20 cm (8 in.) loose-bottomed, deep tin. Press down around the edges.

Prepare the apple filling. Peel, core and slice the apples. Place in a saucepan with the 85 g (3 oz) of demerara sugar and water. Poach gently for 1½ minutes but do not allow the apples to lose their shape. Cool the apples and spread this mixture on top of the pastry in the tin.

Prepare the sponge mixture. Place butter, sugar, flour and eggs in a bowl and beat for 2-3 minutes. Then add the ground almonds and half of the flaked nuts. If the mixture is a little stiff, add 1 dessertsp. of cold water and continue mixing. Spread over the top of the apples and sprinkle with 30 g (1 oz) of flaked or chopped almonds. Bake in the oven at 180 °C (350 °F or regulo 4) for 45-50 minutes.

To make the topping, heat the sugar, lemon juice, honey and Calvados together until bubbling, then brush over the top of the cake. Serve hot.

The Calvados is optional and if cooking for the children can be substituted with a little extra lemon juice.

Serves 8-10

Bread and Apple Pudding

There is more to making a bread and butter pudding than many will acknowledge. The secret lies in not using too much bread; otherwise the pudding will become stodgy. It is always difficult to be exact with the amount of bread as dish sizes vary but I feel it looks more attractive with the bread layered over the top.

This autumn version of bread and butter pudding is just delicious, served straight from the oven with a golden, crisp crust. For the health conscious, and many of us are today, try using starch-reduced bread and semi-skimmed milk.

4 slices of fresh white bread
2 Bramley apples, cut into slices
570 ml (1 pint) milk
55 g (2 oz) caster sugar
4 egg yolks
55 g (2 oz) caster sugar
½ teasp. ground cinnamon
55 g (2 oz) sultanas

Heat the milk to warm but not boiling point. Pour over the egg yolks which have been lightly whisked with caster sugar. Peel and slice the apples and toss in a bowl with the sultanas, caster sugar and cinnamon. Arrange the bread in a well-greased ovenproof dish and sprinkle with the apples and sultanas. Next, pour the custard over the bread and fruit and arrange the remaining slices of bread across the top in an overlapping fashion. Leave to soak for half an hour, then bake at 180 °C (350 °F or regulo 4) for 20-25 minutes or until crisp and golden-brown on top.

Soda Bread with Cinnamon and Apple

450 g (1 lb) plain flour
1 teasp. salt
½ teasp. cinnamon
1 teasp. baking soda
1 teasp. sugar (optional)
1 cooking apple, diced
570 ml (1 pint) buttermilk or sour milk

Sieve the dry ingredients into a large bowl. Add the diced apple. Scoop up handfuls of this and allow to drop back into the bowl to aerate the mixture. Add enough buttermilk to make a soft dough. Working quickly, as the buttermilk and soda are already reacting, knead the dough lightly: too much handling will toughen it, while too little means it won't rise properly.

Form a round loaf about as thick as your fist. Place it on a lightly floured baking sheet and cut a cross on the top with a floured knife. Put at once to bake near the top of a pre-heated oven at 200 °C (400 °F or regulo 6) for 30–45 minutes. When baked, the loaf will sound hollow when rapped on the bottom. Wrap immediately in a clean tea-towel to prevent the crust from hardening too much.

Toffee Apple Tart

Apples are rarely improved by prolonged cooking or by complication. It is usually best to cook them briefly. I adapt this tart to whichever fruit is in season.

225 g (8 oz) puff pastry or shortcrust pastry
6 well-flavoured eating apples
70 ml (⅛ pint) cider or apple liqueur such as Calvados
30 g (1 oz) caster sugar
Icing sugar and cinnamon to serve

Toffee
55 g (2 oz) butter
115 g (4 oz) demerara sugar
Pinch of cream of tartar
4 dessertsp. water

Roll out the pastry very thinly and cut a disc approximately 20 cm (8 in.) in diameter using a plate as a guide. Place on a dampened baking sheet and prick all over with a fork.

Peel, core and slice the apples, removing the skin if desired and toss in the cider or liqueur for several minutes. Arrange the fruit on top of the pastry disc, fanning it out and doming it up in the middle. Sprinkle with caster sugar and bake in the oven at 190 °C (375 °F or regulo 5) for 20-25 minutes.

Next prepare the toffee. Melt the butter in a pan, add the brown sugar, cream of tartar and water and after dissolving the sugar, boil rapidly until the toffee turns a thick golden-brown. Allow to cool slightly, then drizzle lightly over the top of the apples. Allow to cool further and harden a little before dusting with icing sugar and cinnamon.

Serve hot with ice cream.

Serves 8

Very Irish Potato Apple Cake

This is a very traditional Irish dish and one I often make as a comforting snack. I like to serve it lightly buttered and dusted with caster sugar. It tastes even better if you warm it in the oven until the butter is melted.

225 g (½ lb) cooked potatoes, finely mashed
2 cooking apples, peeled and finely diced
½ teasp. cinnamon
30 g (1 oz) demerara sugar
1 dessertsp. lemon juice
½ teasp. salt and pepper
30 g (1 oz) melted butter
55 g (2 oz) flour
Butter and caster sugar to serve

Into a bowl place the diced apple, cinnamon, demerara sugar and lemon juice. Cover and leave to sit while preparing the potato cake. This dish is easier to make if the potatoes are still warm. Cook and finely mash the potatoes, add the salt, pepper and gradually work in the flour until the dough becomes very pliable. On a floured board roll out the dough 5 mm (4 in.) thick and cut into circles approximately 7.5 cm (3 in.) in diameter. Cover one round with the apple mixture, dampen the edge and cover with the second piece. Seal the edges with a fork or by pinching with your fingers. Cook on the griddle until golden-brown and cooked. Spread with melted butter and caster sugar.

Alternatively this dish can also be cooked in the oven at 190 °C (375 °F or regulo 5) for 20 minutes.

Braised Hot Pickled Red Cabbage with Apples

1 medium red cabbage, shredded
340 g (12 oz) cooking apples, peeled and sliced
1 onion, finely diced
1 dessertsp. cooking oil
115 g (4 oz) demerara sugar
Pinch of salt and pepper
570 ml (1 pint) water or vegetable stock
140 ml (¼ pint) red wine
2 dessertsp. cider vinegar
55 g (2 oz) raisins

In a large pan, sauté the onions in the oil, add the cabbage, apples, sugar, salt and pepper and toss. Next add the stock, red wine, cider vinegar and stir well. Place the lid on the pan and simmer gently for 1-1¼ hours until tender. This dish can also be braised in the oven. Ten minutes before serving add the raisins, allow them to plump up nicely, then serve hot.

Hot Apple Cider

Here's a lovely drink for Christmas morning or for a cold wintry day. This cider can be served to children—just leave out the brandy.

1.1 L (2 pints) apple juice or cider
4 whole cloves
3 cinnamon sticks
2 lemons, thinly sliced
30 g (1 oz) caster sugar
140 ml (¼ pint) brandy or Calvados
1 red apple, cut into fine slices ⎫
Lemon cut in fine slices ⎭ **to serve**

Combine the cloves, cinnamon, lemon slices, apple juice and sugar in a large saucepan. Simmer for 10-15 minutes until the flavours have blended. Strain, then return the liquid to the pan with the brandy. Bring to bubbling point and serve with lemon and apple slices.

Serves 10

9 *Pat a Cake, Pat a Cake*

Cakes need that special ingredient—light handling—so if I'm not in the mood to bake a cake then I don't bother.

I firmly believe there is more to cake-making than the careful balance of ingredients, accurate weighing, correct size of tin and of course the correct temperature and position in the oven.

The first cake I ever baked was a plain butter sandwich filled with raspberry jam and dusted with caster sugar. I won't say just how many years ago that was but I was so delighted with the result that my love of cakes has continued to grow.

I am not one for over-elaborate cakes unless it's for a special occasion such as Easter or Mothering Sunday. In fact I much prefer cakes with simple decoration or even one where the topping and cake are cooked together.

Today there is such a variety of flours, fats, sugars, egg size, raising agents, tins, ovens, and paper to line tins with, that even the most knowledgeable of cooks must get confused occasionally. Even cakes with the same ingredients will end up with a totally different texture depending upon how and in what order the ingredients are incorporated into the recipes. Likewise, the amount of dough in a tin will affect how the cake bakes.

I like to flour or sugar tins after greasing to help the cake 'catch' at the sides; otherwise the slippery surface will prevent the cake from rising to its full volume. Cakes which require more than 45 minutes cooking time will usually need to be covered after 30 minutes with greased paper to prevent over-browning.

Many of the cakes in this section freeze well as the recipes are simple and unfussy. The texture of defrosted cakes can often be improved by placing them in a microwave on low power for a few seconds or in the oven at medium to low heat for no longer than 2-3 minutes, provided the cake is not iced or filled.

I have included a wide variety of cakes in this section. My favourite yoghurt cake is very popular today but remember, this recipe requires baking soda used with plain flour, as an acid ingredient such as yoghurt or soured cream can cause the cake to rise too high and crack. The cinnamon tea cake is a quick, simple cake made almost by the all-in-one method. Beekeeper's cake with nutmeg is our family standby and one which keeps very well in an air-tight tin. Fruit cakes are delicious at any time of the year so I have included one for a light sweet cake, our farmhouse fruit cake, and a very special one, the recipe for my wedding cake.

Simnel Cake

Simnel cakes were originally baked in two layers with a filling of almond paste in between. If serving this traditional cake for Easter it can be decorated with eleven marzipan balls to represent the apostles without Judas. The cake can of course be decorated with almond paste, icing and colourful spring flowers.

285 g (10 oz) raisins
285 g (10 oz) golden sultanas
115 g (4 oz) chopped glacé fruits
70 ml (⅛ pint) dry sherry
225 g (8 oz) butter
225 g (8 oz) soft brown sugar
4 eggs, lightly whisked
225 g (8 oz) plain flour
½ teasp. baking powder
Rind of 1 lemon, finely grated
1 teasp. mixed spice
½ teasp. nutmeg
85 g (3 oz) ground almonds
Few drops of vanilla essence

Almond paste
170 g (6 oz) ground almonds
85 g (3 oz) caster sugar
85 g (3 oz) icing sugar
A little almond essence and vanilla flavouring
1 egg

Soak the raisins, sultanas and glacé fruit overnight in the sherry. Prepare a round, deep 23 cm (9 in.) tin by lining well with either waxed or grease-proof paper.

Cream the butter and soft brown sugar until light and fluffy. Then alternately add the lightly whisked eggs with vanilla essence and sieved flour. I find it a good idea to add a little flour before the eggs; this prevents the mixture curdling. Add the eggs and flour in three to four additions and add the baking powder with the last of the flour. Next add the finely grated lemon rind, mixed spice, nutmeg and ground almonds, mixing well. Finally add all the marinated fruit and ensure it is evenly dispersed throughout the cake.

To make the almond paste, mix the ground almonds with the icing sugar and caster sugar. Add the vanilla flavouring and almond essence and sufficient beaten egg to give a pliable but not sticky paste. Cover a board with a little sieved icing sugar, turn out the paste and knead until smooth. Roll out and cut out a circle the size of the tin. If using almond paste to decorate the top of the cake, repeat this process. I like to allow at least a 170 g (6 oz) quantity of almond paste for the centre and the same for the top. The layer in the centre of the cake should be approximately 1–1½ cm (½–¾ in.) thick.

Spoon half the mixture into the lined tin and level the top. Place the layer of almond paste on top and finally the remainder of the cake mixture and again level the top. Bake in the oven at 160 °C (325 °F or regulo 3) for 2½-3 hours or until cooked and firm. Leave the cake in the tin for 15 minutes to cool before turning out to prevent the cake from splitting at the marzipan layer. When cold, decorate the cake as you wish.

This cake can be decorated in several ways. Use almond paste to create a traditional Simnel cake. Or cover with almond paste and royal icing, then decorate with candied spring flowers to create a cake which is ideal for Mothering Sunday.

Our Farmhouse Fruit Cake

225 g (8 oz) raisins
225 g (8 oz) sultanas
115 g (4 oz) currants
Pinch of of mixed spice
Pinch of nutmeg
Zest of 1 orange and 1 lemon
1 dessertsp. marmalade
225 g (8 oz) mixed glacé fruit, chopped
225 g (8 oz) butter
225 g (8 oz) soft brown sugar
4 large eggs, beaten
½ teasp. vanilla essence
170 g (6 oz) plain flour
115 g (4 oz) self-raising cake flour
55 g (2 oz) ground almonds
115 g (4 oz) blanched almonds, split
Pinch of salt

Mix the raisins, sultanas, currants, spice, nutmeg, zest of orange and lemon, marmalade and chopped mixed glacé fruits. Stir well to mix the flavours and set aside. Next prepare a 20 cm (8 in.) square cake tin, lining well with greaseproof paper and grease with lard or oil but not butter. Cakes tend to brown more if butter is used.

Cream the butter and sugar together until light and fluffy. To this, alternately add eggs, vanilla essence, salt and flour, finishing off with ground almonds and the last of the flour. Mix in the fruit and spice mixture with half the almonds. Place the cake mixture in the prepared tin, smooth on top and arrange the remaining split almonds over the top. Sprinkle a little cold water (1 dessertsp.) over the top of the cake with a pastry brush. This helps prevent it becoming over-browned. Bake in the oven at 160 °C (325 °F or regulo 3) for 2½-3 hours or until a skewer is withdrawn dry from the centre of the cake. Half way through cooking, I find it a good idea to place a sheet of greaseproof paper on top of the cake.

Victorian Lemon Cake
with Elderflower and Lemon Curd

This is a one-stage recipe. Mix the four main ingredients together—fat, sugar, flour, and eggs—a speedy and excellent result. This cake can be sandwiched together with jam but the use of lemon and elderflower curd transforms the flavour.

170 g (6 oz) soft margarine
170 g (6 oz) caster sugar
200 g (7 oz) self-raising flour
1 teasp. baking powder
4 small eggs or 3 large eggs, lightly beaten
2 lemons, to make zest and 1 dessertsp. lemon juice
Icing sugar to decorate

Grease two 20 cm (8 in.) sandwich tins, then dust with a sprinkling of caster sugar.

Using a mixer, beat the margarine, caster sugar, flour, baking powder and lightly beaten eggs until light, white and creamy. Add the finely grated zest of 2 lemons and 1 dessertsp. of lemon juice. Be careful not to add any extra lemon juice or this will cause the cake to crack. If the mixture is a little stiff, add water (no more than 1 dessertsp.). Otherwise the cake will become hard.

Turn the mixture into the two sandwich tins and bake at 190 °C (375 °F or regulo 5) for 25-30 minutes. When ready, the cake should be golden-brown and have shrunk away from the edges. Cool in the tins for 2-3 minutes before turning out on to a cooling tray.

Elderflower Lemon Curd
2 dessertsp. elderflower cordial or
**   liquid from infused elderflower heads**
3 eggs, beaten
170 g (6 oz) caster sugar
85 g (3 oz) butter, cubed
3 lemons

Place a bowl containing the beaten eggs, sugar, cubes of butter and the fine rind and juice of 3 lemons over a saucepan of hot water and whisk continually until the lemon curd shows signs of thickening. Be careful not to let the water boil, otherwise the lemon curd will curdle. Remove from the heat and stir in the elderflower cordial (this can be bought quite easily nowadays) or instead infuse 4-5 washed elderflower heads in 140 ml (¼ pint) boiling water with 2 dessertsp. of caster sugar. Leave to infuse for at least half an hour. Strain the liquid and place in a saucepan and heat until it reduces to a concentrated 2-3 dessertsp.

Use the lemon curd to sandwich this delicious cake together. If liked, a little whipped cream or yoghurt can also be spread between the layers. Serve cold dusted with icing sugar.

My Favourite Yoghurt Cake

This yoghurt cake will store extremely well and even freeze. Try varying the flavour by using a different flavoured yoghurt, such as banana. Cook in a 900 g (2 lb) loaf tin or 20 cm (8 in.) round deep-sided tin.

170 g (6 oz) plain flour
1 teasp. baking soda
85 g (3 oz) butter, softened, or unsaturated margarine
140 g (5 oz) caster sugar
2 large eggs, separated
1 small carton low-fat yoghurt
Few drops vanilla essence

Preheat the oven to 180 °C (350 °F or regulo 4).

Sieve the flour and baking soda into a large bowl. In a separate bowl, cream the fat and sugar until light and fluffy, then add the well-beaten egg yolks, mixing well. Add the sieved flour mixture and yoghurt alternately in approximately three additions. Add the vanilla essence. Beat the egg whites until stiff, then carefully fold into the mixture. Pour into the prepared tin and bake in the centre rack of the oven for 1¼ hours approximately until a golden-brown colour and the tester comes out clean.

Beekeeper's Cake with Nutmeg

This is one of the simplest cakes I know and a great standby to have 'in the tins'. The topping for this cake is warmed honey and nutmeg drizzled over the cake while still warm.

3 eggs
115 g (4 oz) caster sugar or soft brown sugar
115 g (4 oz) melted butter
4 dessertsp. honey
200 g (7 oz) self-raising flour

Topping
2 dessertsp. warmed honey
Pinch of nutmeg

Line a round 20 cm (8 in.) deep-sided cake tin or a 900 g (2 lb) loaf tin. This cake cooks best in a shallow tin. Beat the eggs and sugar together until light, fluffy and holding their shape.

In a saucepan or in a microwave very gently soften the butter, then cool. Pour the cooled butter and honey into the egg mixture, fold through, then add the sifted flour, folding gently to keep the cake light. Pour into the prepared tin and bake at 180 °C (350 °F or regulo 4) until cooked, approximately ¾ hour. Allow to cool slightly before topping the cake with warmed honey and a sprinkling of nutmeg.

Cinnamon Tea Cake

85 g (3 oz) butter
55 g (2 oz) caster sugar
1 teasp. vanilla essence
115 g (4 oz) self-raising flour, sieved
2 small eggs, beaten
70 ml (⅛ pint) milk

Topping
15 g (½ oz) butter, melted
1 teasp. ground cinnamon
30 g (1 oz) demerara sugar

Beat the butter, sugar and vanilla essence in a small bowl until light and fluffy for approximately 5 minutes. Fold in the sieved flour, egg and milk and mix until smooth. Transfer to a well-greased deep 20 cm (8 in.) tin and bake at 180 °C (350 °F or regulo 4) for approximately 30 minutes. When cooked, turn out onto a tray and while still, warm brush the top with melted butter and sprinkle with the mixed sugar and cinnamon. If liked, this cake can be slightly caramelised on top by placing below a grill for just a few minutes but do watch it carefully.

Wholewheat Sponge Cake with Butterscotch Filling

This is a rather light-textured wholewheat cake. The flavour of the filling can easily be varied but I find the fudge filling particularly good.

4 eggs, separated
115 g (4 oz) soft light brown sugar
1 tablesp. honey
½ teasp. vanilla essence
1 tablesp. warm water
55 g (2 oz) wholewheat flour }
85 g (3 oz) plain flour } mixed

Fudge Filling
85 g (3 oz) butter
140 g (5 oz) soft brown sugar
½ teasp. vanilla essence
1 tablesp. cream

30 g (1 oz) icing sugar, to decorate

Over a bowl of warm water, beat the egg yolks with the sugar until light and foamy. Fold in the honey, vanilla essence and water. Next add the flours and carefully fold in the egg whites. Divide the mixture between 2 greased 20 cm (8 in.) sponge tins and bake at 180 °C (350 °F or regulo 4) for 25-30 minutes until well risen and firm to the touch. When cooked, cool before filling.

To make the filling, melt the butter in a saucepan, add the brown sugar, vanilla essence and cream, stirring until dissolved. Then boil for 2-3 minutes until fudge-like. Allow to cool, then use to sandwich the cakes together. Dust the top with icing sugar.

Berry Berry Fresh Fruit Cake

This is a lovely cake for summertime with the abundance of fresh berries in season. A cake which may also be used as a pudding if served warm with a little eggy custard, whipped cream or fromage frais flavoured with a little fruit purée. Choose fruit which is firm and not over-ripe.

225 g (8 oz) fresh strawberries or raspberries
1 dessertsp. caster sugar
Rind of 1 lemon
170 g (6 oz) butter
170 g (6 oz) soft brown sugar
3 eggs, lightly beaten
170 g (6 oz) self-raising cake flour, sieved
55 g (2 oz) ground almonds
½ teasp. vanilla essence
Icing sugar to dust
Mint and fresh berry leaves to decorate

Place the fruit in a bowl. If the berries are small leave whole, if not cut in half. Add 1 dessertsp. of caster sugar and the rind of 1 lemon. Leave the fruits to marinate while preparing the sponge mixture.

Cream the butter and brown sugar until light and fluffy. Then alternately add the beaten egg and sieved flour, adding the ground almonds and vanilla essence with the last of the flour. Add half the fruit to the cake mixture and toss lightly. If the mixture is a little stiff, use 1 dessertsp. water to soften. Transfer to a well-greased 20 cm (8 in.) cake tin, preferably with a loose bottom. Bake at 190 °C (375 °F or regulo 5) until risen, brown and firm to the touch, approximately 1 hour. Leave this cake in the tin to cool a little before turning it.

To finish, dust with a little icing sugar or serve with the remaining fresh fruit piled high on top and decorate with mint leaves or fresh berry leaves.

Serves 8-10

Roasted Hazelnut and Rhubarb Cake

225 g (8 oz) rhubarb, cut into small pieces
30 g (1 oz) demerara sugar
170 g (6 oz) butter
170 g (6 oz) soft brown sugar
4 eggs, lightly beaten
200 g (7 oz) self-raising flour, sieved
55 g (2 oz) ground almonds
1 dessertsp. caster sugar to dust the tin

Topping
55 g (2 oz) wholemeal flour
30 g (1 oz) butter
30 g (1 oz) demerara sugar
55 g (2 oz) chopped, roasted hazelnuts

In a small bowl prepare the topping by rubbing the butter into the wholemeal flour until it looks crumbly. Next add the demerara sugar and roasted hazelnuts.

Wash and slice the rhubarb and toss in 1 oz demerara sugar to sweeten. Prepare a 18 cm (7 in.) loose-bottomed tin by greasing lightly and dusting with 1 dessertsp. caster sugar. Cream the butter and soft brown sugar, then alternately add the beaten eggs and sieved flour. With the last of the flour add the ground almonds. If the mixture is a little on the stiff side add 1 tablesp. of cold water and mix. Place half of the sponge mixture into the tin, sprinkle the sugared rhubarb on top, then cover with the remainder of the sponge mixture. Flatten, then sprinkle with the topping and bake in the oven at 180 °C (350 °F or regulo 4) for approximately 1 hour.

My Wedding Cake

I am asked so often for a fruit cake recipe suitable for a wedding cake that I decided to publish the recipe of my own wedding cake for that very special day. Following tradition, the top tier was put away into storage and used for the Christening of our first born.

The average size wedding cake consists of 3 tiers: 30 cm (12 in.), 23 cm (9 in.) and 15 cm (6 in.) and this should serve about 150 people, bearing in mind that the servings are generally small. The quantity given below is for a 23 cm (9 in.) tin for the middle tier and the quantities can be adjusted for the larger or smaller tin. Use the quantity of butter as a guideline and adjust the quantities accordingly for the size of cake you are making.

For a 15 cm (6 in.) tin, use 115 g (4 oz) butter
For a 23 cm (9 in.) tin, use 225 g (8 oz) butter
For a 30 cm (12 in.) tin, use 340 g (12 oz) butter

Fruit Mixture
450 g (1 lb) sultanas
340 g (12 oz) raisins

170 g (6 oz) red and green glacé cherries, cut in half
55 g (2 oz) apricots, finely chopped
55 g (2 oz) crystallised pineapple, chopped
140 ml (¼ pint) ginger ale
140 ml (¼ pint) sherry, brandy or rum

Cake Mixture
225 g (8 oz) butter
225 g (8 oz) soft brown sugar
4 eggs, well beaten
255 g (9 oz) plain flour
55 g (2 oz) ground almonds
1 teasp. mixed spice
½ teasp. nutmeg
1 teasp. honey
¼ teasp. vanilla essence
¼ teasp. almond essence

Cooking time for 23 cm (9 in.) tin: oven temperature of 180 °C (350 °F or regulo 4) for the first hour, then reduce to 160 °C (325 °F or regulo 3) for 2 ½-3 hours or until cooked.

Prepare the tin by greasing well and lining with waxed or silicone paper. Place a band of double thickness brown paper, newspaper or greaseproof paper around the tin on the outside.

To prepare the fruit wash the sultanas and raisins in water, dry, then place in a bowl with the halved cherries, finely chopped apricots and pineapple. Pour the ginger ale and spirits over the fruit and leave covered for 24 hours until the fruit absorbs the liquid. Stir occasionally.

To prepare the cake mixture: cream the butter and soft brown sugar well. Either light or dark brown sugar can be used but this will affect the finished colour of the cake. Add the well-beaten eggs and flour alternately, mixing well between additions. Add in 3 or 4 stages and with the remainder of the flour add the ground almonds, spices, honey and essences. Mix well, then add the steeped fruit. If any of the liquid remains in the bottom of the fruit bowl, add it in at the end and mix well.

Transfer to the cake tin and place on the lower to middle shelf and bake. After the first hour I find it a good idea to place a circle of greaseproof paper on top of the cake to prevent it from browning. When cooked, do not remove from the tin for at least 1 hour. Store well.

This cake can be covered with almond paste and decorated when required.

10 *When there's Nothing in the Tins*

In the country there is almost a hint of embarrassment if there is 'nothing in the tins' when friends drop in. How often have we all been caught out? Local hospitality expects at least a cup of tea and something to eat, yet how sad it is that some protest that tea and biscuits are unnecessary extras and only for putting on weight.

Baking is losing its interest in many homes yet I feel it's part of a way of life, and today filling the tins can be speedy, healthy and fun.

Foolproof pancakes are so quick to make either in a pan or on the griddle, and toasted. Buttered scones with home-made jam are hot favourites and loved by all.

Strudel made using bought filo pastry can be either sweet or savoury and I have included two ideas—one for rhubarb and raisin, the other for Stilton, apple and walnut. These can be cut into slices and re-heated easily. Muffins are great for children to make and again can be either sweet or savoury; after they are cooked there is always the tin to run your finger around.

Other favourites of mine are a cracking good cake, speedy date cake made with potatoes or Irish freckled tea loaf which has to be one of the quickest and most successful I have ever made, and of course pavlova, that favourite meringue which stores so well in a tin for 2-3 weeks.

Blackberry and Apple Crêpes

Crêpes or pancakes can be made in minutes and children love them. Try filling them with apple, blackberries and fromage frais for a really tasty treat.

Crêpes
115 g (4 oz) flour
Pinch of salt
280 ml (½ pint) milk
2 eggs, beaten
2 tablesp. oil or melted butter for frying
Caster sugar to coat

Blackberry and Apple Sauce
225 g (8 oz) fresh or frozen blackberries
1 apple, cut into slices
4 tablesp. caster sugar
1 dessertsp. lemon juice
1 dessertsp. cornflour blended with water (if needed)

Filling
1 dessertsp. fromage frais
2 dessertsp. blackberry and apple sauce

Sieve the flour and salt into a bowl, and make a well in the centre. Mix the beaten eggs with the milk, then whisk into the flour. Mix until smooth and the consistency of single cream. Leave the batter to settle before cooking. Brush a crêpe pan or frying pan with oil, adding sufficient batter to cover the pan. Tilt the pan until evenly coated, cook until brown, turn and cook the other side. Turn onto a plate and dust with a little caster sugar. Continue until all the batter has been used. Keep the crêpes warm.

To make the sauce, poach the blackberries, slices of apple, sugar and lemon juice until the apple becomes soft. If using frozen berries the sauce may become thin. This can easily be thickened using 1 dessertsp. of cornflour blended with cold water. Add to the pan and heat through. Fill the crêpes with 1 dessertsp. fromage frais, and spoon 2 dessertsp. of the warm sauce on top. Roll up and serve immediately.

Plain Scones with Strawberry Jam

There is no secret in this recipe, for the making of scones is all to do with the mixing.

225 g (8 oz) self-raising cake flour
Pinch of salt
45 g (1½ oz) fat or butter
30 g (1 oz) caster sugar
1 large egg, lightly beaten
8-10 tablesp. milk (approx.)

Sieve the flour and salt together, cut and rub in the fat, add the sugar and mix well. Next add the egg and milk. I find the success in scone-making lies in adding the milk quickly to the mixture. If added slowly, the scones become crumbly and close-textured. Roll out on a lightly floured surface to 2 cm (¾ in.) thick and using a small cutter (approximately 2 in.) cut out the scones. Place on a lightly floured baking sheet, brush with milk or a lightly beaten egg and bake at 220 °C (425 °F or regulo 7) for 12-15 minutes. Cool the scones by wrapping in a tea towel. I like to serve these scones lightly buttered with home-made strawberry jam.

Granny Bristow's Griddle Bread

My mother-in-law, known to the family as Granny Bristow, always has 'something in her tins' as she can make the most delicious griddle bread in minutes, using a handful of this and a little bit of that. With a little gentle persuasion I encouraged her to let me measure the ingredients so I can share it with you.

115 g (4 oz) plain flour, sieved
225 g (8 oz) coarse wheaten meal flour
1 teasp. salt
1 teasp. baking soda
425 ml (¾ pint) buttermilk (approx.) or 425 ml (¾ pint) sweet
    milk and 1 teasp. white vinegar

Sieve the plain flour, then mix all the dry ingredients well by hand to get as much air as possible into the bread at this stage. Add the buttermilk but be careful not to make the mixture too soft; otherwise the bread will have raggy edges. Mix to a smooth dough, then turn out onto a floured board, shape into a round and cut into 4 farls.

Have the griddle pre-heated and sprinkled with flour. Cook the farls on the griddle for approximately 5 minutes on each side. When they are ready they will sound hollow when tapped.

Irish Freckled Tea Loaf

This cake cooks in either a 90 g (2 lb) loaf tin or 20 cm (8 in.) diameter round tin, lined.

225 g (8 oz) sultanas
½ teasp. mixed spice
7 cherries, chopped
7 walnuts, chopped
115 g (4 oz) soft brown sugar
140 ml (¼ pint) cold tea
140 g (5 oz) margarine or butter
2 eggs, lightly beaten
225 g (8 oz) self-raising flour

Place the sultanas, spice, cherries, walnuts, soft brown sugar, tea and fat into a saucepan, bring to the boil then turn off the heat immediately and leave to cool. Beat the eggs separately, then add to the mixture slowly with the sieved flour. Mix well then bake in the oven 190 °C (375 °F or regulo 5) for approximately 1 hour.

Leave to cool in the tin before turning out.

Banana Tea Bread

Bananas are probably one of my favourite fruits and in this recipe they help create a tea bread which is soft-textured and moist.

115 g (4 oz) butter or margarine
115 g (4 oz) granulated sugar
2 ripe bananas, mashed coarsely
115 g (4 oz) self-raising flour, sieved
½ teasp. baking powder
1 egg, beaten
85 g (3 oz) wholemeal flour

Cream the butter and sugar, then mix in the mashed bananas. Next add the sieved self-raising flour and baking powder with the beaten egg and finally the wholemeal flour. Turn into a well-greased and base-lined 450 g (1 lb) loaf tin. Bake in the middle shelf of the oven at 180 °C (350 °F or regulo 4) for approximately 45-50 minutes until the loaf is firm and showing signs of shrinking away from the sides of the tin.

Speedy Date Cake

This is a useful cake if you are asked to produce cakes or buns en masse for a special function. It is very economical as it uses potato—that versatile tuber—as one of the main ingredients. They also add texture. I prefer to make this cake in a shallow, rectangular tin, then cut into squares when cold.

170 g (6 oz) margarine or butter
225 g (8 oz) demerara sugar
85 g (3 oz) potatoes, cooked and mashed
½ teasp. vanilla essence
2 eggs, beaten
225 g (8 oz) chopped dates
140 g (5 oz) self-raising cake flour
30 g (1 oz) walnuts, finely chopped

Cream together the margarine and sugar, add the sieved cooked potatoes, vanilla essence and well-beaten eggs. Fold in the dates, flour and finely chopped walnuts. Transfer to a greased baking tin, approximately 28 cm x 18 cm (11 in. x 7 in.). Bake for 25-30 minutes at 180 °C (350 °F or regulo 4) until golden-brown.

Hot Cross Irish Soda Bread with Herbs

225 g (8 oz) self-raising soda bread flour
½ teasp. salt
1 tablesp. parsley, finely chopped
½ teasp. thyme, finely chopped
1 egg, lightly beaten
140 ml (¼ pint) buttermilk (approx.)
115 g (4 oz) shortcrust pastry
To brush: 1 egg, lightly beaten

Sieve the dry ingredients into a bowl. Add the herbs, the lightly beaten egg and sufficient buttermilk to mix to a soft but not sticky dough. Turn onto a well-floured surface, divide the mixture into 12, and shape into rounds. Place on a floured baking sheet. Roll out the shortcrust pastry to 1 cm (¼ in.) thick, cut into fine strips and use to criss-cross the top of each little soda bread. Brush with beaten egg—you may find it easier to get the pastry to stick if the soda rounds are brushed with a little egg first.

Alternatively, a large soda bread can be made by turning out the dough and shaping into one large round. Remember to put a large cross on top: this is supposed to let the fairies out! Bake at 220 °C (425 °F or regulo 7)—a large soda takes 25 minutes, 15 minutes for smaller rounds.

Crunchy Savoury Loaf

225 g (8 oz) self-raising flour
½ level teasp. salt
½ level teasp. paprika
30 g (1 oz) butter or margarine
115 g (4 oz) celery, finely chopped
115 g (4 oz) cheddar cheese, grated
1 tablesp. parsley, chopped
140 ml (¼ pint) milk

Sieve flour, salt and paprika into a bowl. Rub in the butter, stir in the celery, cheese and parsley. Reserve a little cheese for the top. Mix to a soft dough with the milk, place in a 450 g (1 lb) loaf tin. Brush top with milk. Bake at 190 °C (375 °F or regulo 5) for approximately ¾ hour.

Remove from the tin and wrap in a tea towel until cool.

Mother McKeag's Bacon Muffins

This amazing lady, known to everyone as Mother McKeag, has the 'recipe for life' at her fingertips. In her own special way, she feeds body and soul. These are her delicious bacon muffins.

85 g (3 oz) back bacon
225 g (8 oz) self-raising flour
1 teasp. baking powder
1 tablesp. parsley, chopped
2 eggs, beaten
115 g (4 oz) butter, melted and cooled
140 ml (¼ pint) milk

Cut the rind and excess fat off the bacon, finely chop and cook until crispy. Sieve the flour and baking powder into a bowl. Stir in the chopped parsley and bacon. Pour in the beaten egg, melted butter and milk to form a dropping consistency. Spoon the mixture into 12 muffin tins or deep patty tins.

Bake in a pre-heated oven at 190 °C (375 °F or regulo 5) for 15-20 minutes. Serve warm. To freeze, pack into bags and use within 2 months.

Makes about 12

Spiced Wholemeal Biscuits

These pretty little biscuits can be baked by the children themselves. This is a foolproof dough and great biscuits to have 'in the tins'. By the use of animal cutters you can vary their shapes.

115 g (4 oz) butter, softened
55 g (2 oz) caster sugar
85 g (3 oz) plain flour
85 g (3 oz) wholemeal flour
½ teasp. ground cinnamon powder
Icing sugar to coat

Cream the butter and sugar together until light and fluffy. Work in the plain and wholemeal flours and the cinnamon powder. Mix until the dough forms a soft ball. Chill in the fridge for at least 15-20 minutes before rolling out 1 cm (½ in.) thick and cut out using a lightly floured cutter. Place on a lightly floured baking sheet and bake at 180 °C (350 °F or regulo 4) for 15-20 minutes. Cool on a wire rack and serve dusted with icing sugar. These little biscuits can be decorated using glacé cherries for eyes and buttons.

Fresh Fruit Pavlova

Meringue
3 large egg whites
170 g (6 oz) caster sugar
1 level teasp. cornflour
1 teasp. white vinegar
½ teasp. vanilla essence (optional)

280 ml (½ pint) whipped cream or yoghurt
340 g (12 oz) assorted fresh fruits, sliced

Line a baking sheet with lightly greased/oiled greaseproof paper or non-stick baking parchment. Into a large, clean, dry, cool bowl add the separated egg whites ensuring there is no trace of egg yolk. Beat the whites at this stage using a hand whisk or electric mixer, until the mixture is very stiff and forms peaks. It is important not to rush this process. Next add the sugar, folding gently, approximately 30 g (1 oz) at a time. A long, slow and very gentle addition of the sugar is very important, folding well between each addition. I find it easier to carry out this stage by hand as over-mixing can cause a pavlova to have a very crunchy outer crust.

Finally, fold in the cornflour, vinegar and vanilla essence (if being used). Pipe or pile the meringue onto a drawn circle on the baking sheet approximately 20 cm (8 in.).

Ensure the oven is preheated at 150 °C (300 °F or regulo 2), and 5 minutes after you put the pavlova mixture in the oven, turn the temperature down to 140 °C (275 °F or regulo 1). Bake for 1¼-1½ hours. Cook until pale brown and dry, although a little soft in the centre. If possible, turn off the oven when cooked and allow the pavlova to remain in the oven overnight to avoid sinking in the middle.

When cold, peel off the paper, place on a serving dish. At this stage the meringue will probably crack and sink a little. Decorate with cream, yoghurt or fromage frais and assorted seasonal fruits.

A Cracking Good Cake

It was Escoffier who said 'The greatest dishes are the simplest ones'. Today cakes can be fussy, and it is refreshing to come up with one so simple it can be used for afternoon tea or to accompany puddings or trifles.

225 g (8 oz) caster sugar infused with vanilla pod
225 g (8 oz) butter
3 eggs, beaten
255 g (9 oz) self-raising flour, sieved
115 g (4 oz) freshly ground almonds
4 tablesp. milk
½ teasp. vanilla essence
Slice of citron peel

Grease and line a 900 g (2 lb) loaf tin with greaseproof paper. Place the vanilla pod into the sugar and leave to infuse for at least 1 hour. Remove the pod.

Cream the butter and sugar until light and fluffy, add the beaten eggs, sieved flour and ground almonds alternately. With the last of the flour, add the milk and vanilla essence. Turn into a prepared tin, flatten the top and decorate with the citron peel. Bake at 180 °C (350 °F or regulo 4) for approximately 1¼ hours. This cake will probably crack on top due to its light texture. Sometimes I like to add 225 g (8 oz) shredded dried apricots to the mixture for a different effect.

Lattice Rhubarb Pie

Fruit pies are always popular but this one is cooked in potato pastry—a crumbly light pastry which is easy to make, and ideal for sweet and savoury dishes.

Pastry
225 g (8 oz) plain flour
85 g (3 oz) potatoes, peeled, cooked and sieved
45 g (1½ oz) margarine
45 g (1½ oz) white vegetable fat
Pinch of salt

Filling
4 stalks of young pink rhubarb
55 g (2 oz) demerara sugar
1 dessertsp. sieved cornflour (if needed)

Trim off the rhubarb leaves, cut the stalks into small bite-sized pieces and place in a bowl with the demerara sugar. If the rhubarb is full of moisture, sprinkle 1 dessertsp. of sieved cornflour over it before cooking. This will help thicken the juices and prevent the pie from becoming soggy.

To prepare the pastry, place all the ingredients in a bowl, mix with a fork: do not add water. Alternatively, a food processor can be used. Divide the mixture into ⅓ and ⅔, then roll ⅔ of the pastry to line a tin or plate. Pile the rhubarb on top and finish off the pie with lattice strips made from the remaining ⅓ of the pastry.

Bake in the oven at 190 °C (375 °F or regulo 5) for 20-25 minutes.

Stilton, Apple and Walnut Strudel

1 large packet of puff pastry
1 egg, lightly beaten
225 g (8 oz) Stilton cheese

Filling
2 cooking apples, finely chopped
115 g (4 oz) walnuts, finely chopped

Roll out the puff pastry (30 cm x 25 cm/12 in. x 10 in. approximately) on a lightly floured board. Brush around the edges with the lightly beaten egg. Prepare the filling, mixing the 225 g (8 oz) crumbled Stilton cheese with the finely chopped cooking apples. I prefer to leave the skin on the apples. Finally, add the finely chopped walnuts and mix well.

Transfer the filling onto the pastry, pat down well, then roll up either into one large roll (or into sausage roll sizes, if preferred). Tuck in the ends, then shape into a log. Cut several slits on top, brush with beaten egg, decorate and bake in the oven at 220 °C (425 °F or regulo 7) for 10 minutes. Then reduce the temperature to 190 °C (375 °F or regulo 5) until cooked, about 10 minutes.

Rhubarb and Raisin Strudel

If I really feel like a challenge I'll tackle strudel pastry and if not, I simply use the packet sheets of filo pastry which work equally well and are tasty if you brush between the sheets with a little melted butter before cooking.

Filling
225 g (8 oz) rhubarb, cut into pieces
Rind and juice of ½ freshly squeezed orange
115 g (4 oz) muscatel raisins
55 g (2 oz) demerara sugar

10 sheets of filo pastry
30 g (1 oz) melted butter
1 egg
Icing sugar to coat

To make the filling poach the rhubarb pieces in a pan with the orange juice and rind, muscatel raisins, and demerara sugar until the rhubarb shows signs of softening. Leave to cool.

Brush a sheet of pastry with melted butter, place another sheet on top and continue this process until all the sheets are piled on top of each other. This also helps to make the pastry waterproof and stops the fruit juices leaking through. Next pile the poached rhubarb along one side of the pastry and roll up, tucking in the ends. If you brush the strudel with a little beaten egg it will help to glaze and seal it. Lay on a baking sheet with the sealed edge downwards. Sprinkle with a little demerara sugar and bake at 190 °C (375 °F or regulo 5) for 20-25 minutes until golden-brown and crisp. Dust with a little icing sugar when cooked and still warm.

Foolproof Pancakes

This is a great recipe where the basic pancake mixture can be made in advance and stored in an air-tight jar for several weeks. When making pancakes, this basic mixture only requires the addition of eggs and milk. It does not require settling time before cooking.

Basic Pancake Mixture
450 g (1 lb) plain flour
1 teasp. salt
6 teasp. baking powder
1 teasp. cream of tartar
225 g (8 oz) margarine
30 g (1 oz) dry milk powder

Pancakes
225 g (8 oz) basic pancake mix
1 egg, lightly beaten
425 ml (¾ pint) milk
Caster sugar and lemon juice to serve

Prepare the mix by sieving the flour into a bowl, add the salt and raising agents, then cut and rub in the fat until the mixture resembles fine bread-crumbs. Add the dry milk powder and store in an air-tight container.

To make the pancakes, mix 225 g (8 oz) of the prepared mix with 1 lightly beaten egg and approximately 280 ml (½ pint) of milk. Mix well to form a smooth batter.

Place 1 large dessertsp. of batter onto a pre-heated, lightly oiled griddle pan and cook until the bubbles are bursting evenly. Then turn once and cook for a further 1-1½ minutes. Serve warm, dusted with caster sugar and lemon juice.

Muffins with Chocolate Chips

Here's a basic muffin recipe which I vary depending on what happens to be in the cupboards. Chocolate chip is always a favourite and these muffins can be made in minutes. The secret of any muffin mixture is not to over-beat, but rather to bind the ingredients together.

170 g (6 oz) plain flour
55 g (2 oz) caster sugar
2 teasp. baking powder
½ teasp. salt
85 g (3 oz) chocolate chips
1 egg, lightly beaten
200 ml (7 oz) milk
85 g (3 oz) melted butter

Mix all the dry ingredients together, then add the chocolate chips. In a separate bowl combine the egg, milk, melted butter and mix gently into the dry ingredients. Do not beat. Transfer to individual muffin tins or cases and bake at 190 °C (375 °F or regulo 5) for approximately 20 minutes. Serve hot or cold.

Makes 10-12

11   *Well Preserved*

reserving has to be one of the most satisfying tasks for any cook. The idea of filling up the larder shelves with jams, jellies, cordials, pickles, marmalades and chutneys invades the soul on even the dullest of days.

Preserving is one of the oldest culinary skills but today there is such a variety of ways in which the flavours of the seasons can be trapped in the bottles and jars. Times must have been hard for the cook when the only ways of coping with the seasonal glut were pickling, bottling or salting.

I feel that the best preserves to make are the ones that cannot be bought and I have come up with recipes which can be used in many ways: the apple cordial can be used as a drink but also for flavouring sauces and casseroles; the Canadian tomato pickle makes a perfect partner for terrines, pâtés, cheese or slices of tender ham; windfall pears in port for that instant pudding; or freezer jam which makes a delicious topping for ice cream or rice pudding.

Sun-dried tomatoes have become so useful in many recipes and provided the sun shines they are foolproof to make. No kitchen cupboard would be complete without a pot of home-made strawberry jam, easy to make but often difficult to set if the fruit is not in prime condition. It can transform your home-made scones or even bread and butter.

Apple Cordial

This mildly-flavoured cordial can be stored in screw-top bottles and diluted. I find it invaluable to add a concentrated apple flavour when roasting pork or duck.

1.35 kg (3 lb) apples, chopped
Juice of 1 lemon
570 ml (1 pint) water

285 g (10 oz) granulated sugar
½ teasp. citric acid

Choose those firm rosy-sided apples if you can for this cordial. They will give it a much nicer flavour and colour. Wash and dry the apples, then chop them but be careful to remove any blemishes on over-ripe apples. Place in a large bowl, cover with water and lemon juice and leave to soften, stirring occasionally. Cover and leave for 24 hours.

Transfer to a heavy-based pan and simmer until the fruit becomes soft. Transfer to a jelly bag or a sieve lined with muslin, and strain. Do not speed up the process or the cordial will become cloudy. Return the strained juice to a saucepan, add the sugar and citric acid, bring to almost boiling point and when the sugar has dissolved, leave to cool. Then bottle.

This cordial should be stored in the fridge for up to 1 week before using.

Candied Flowers

The simplest way to candy flowers is to pick a selection of flowers in prime condition. Leave to dry for at least 1 hour then brush each petal with beaten egg white. Sprinkle with caster sugar. Set the flowers aside on a tray in a warm place until bone dry.

They can be stored in an air-tight box for 1-2 weeks.

Rosehip Syrup

Pick the rosehips in late autumn; they are better picked after the first frost of winter. Make the syrup as quickly as possible after picking as they deteriorate rapidly. Pick the tops and tails off the rosehips. Dry carefully so they retain their red colour.

900 g (2 lb) rosehips
Juice of 1 lemon
450 g (1 lb) granulated sugar, warmed

In a blender or food processor whizz the rosehips until very finely chopped. Add to 1.7 L (3 pints) of boiling water and lemon juice, bring back to boiling point, cook for 2 minutes. Then turn off the heat and allow to infuse for 1 hour. Next strain the syrup either through a jelly bag, fine muslin or a sieve. It is important to remove those bristly hairs that surround the seeds. Return the pulp to a large pan with 850 ml (1½ pints) of fresh boiling water, boil again for 2 minutes, turn off the heat as before, allowing to infuse for 10 minutes. Then strain again. Return the syrup to the saucepan one final time, add the warmed sugar (best warmed by placing in a low oven on a baking sheet), dissolve gently (don't be tempted at this stage to turn up the heat). When boiling point is reached, boil for 5 minutes. Over-cooking will spoil the colour. When cooled slightly, pour the syrup into well-sterilised bottles or jars, filling to within 2.5 cm (1 in.) of the top of the jars, and cork.

This syrup is best stored in a fridge or cool place. The colour is best if used within a few weeks but I have stored this syrup throughout last winter, and have only one bottle left. Pour over ice cream or rice pudding. Also makes a refreshing hot drink.

Rhubarb and Lavender Jelly

900 g (2 lb) rhubarb
10 stalks lavender, preferably fresh
Juice of 2 lemons
450 g (1 lb) granulated sugar to each pint of strained liquid

Wash the rhubarb and cut into 2.5 cm (1 in.) chunks. Place in a bowl with the lavender heads and stems, juice of 2 lemons and sufficient cold water to just cover the rhubarb. Leave the flavours to infuse for at least 1 hour, then transfer to a pan and simmer gently until tender.

Strain the rhubarb through muslin or a jelly bag into a bowl. Be careful not to squeeze the bag or the jelly will become cloudy. Measure the strained liquid and allow 450 g (1 lb) sugar to each pint of strained liquid. Bring to the boil and cook rapidly for 10 minutes or until the jelly shows signs of setting. Allow to cool slightly before pouring into clean, sterile jars.

The main crop rhubarb has good setting qualities.

Home-made Strawberry Jam

I always make this variety of strawberry jam as I have a wooded bank near the house which produces an abundance of wild strawberries in June. If you cannot find them wild, then this recipe can be made successfully using your own home-grown variety or the best of the local crop. Even the addition of a handful of wild strawberries to this recipe will improve the flavour and setting quality.

This can be one of the most difficult jams to set as strawberries are low in pectin. Always choose fruit that is in prime condition. Alternatively, commercial pectin can be used.

1.35 kg (3 lb) strawberries
Juice of 1 lemon
1.35 kg (3 lb) granulated sugar, warmed

In a large saucepan, simmer the washed, hulled strawberries and lemon juice for approximately 5 minutes. Add the warmed sugar (place on a baking sheet in a low oven just to take the chill off it before adding). Stir the jam over a low heat until the sugar has dissolved, turn up the heat and boil rapidly for about 15 minutes until the jam shows signs of setting by the wrinkle test. If using a thermometer, this should happen at 105 °C (221 °F). Remove from the heat and allow to cool slightly. Remove the scum from the jam using a spoon. The fruit will disperse better throughout this jam if it is cooled slightly before potting. Pour into sterile jars, cover with waxed discs and seal.

Makes 2.25-2.70 kg (5-6 lb)

Freezer Jam

This jam retains its bright colour much better, has a strong fruit flavour and is not too sweet. I like to use it as an instant sauce for ice cream or baked rice pudding. Strawberry is my favourite and, I feel, the most successful version, but I have tried making it with blackberries and apricots with equally pleasing results.

450 g (1 lb) strawberries, hulled and cut in half
680 g (1½ lb) sugar
70 ml (⅛ pint) liquid pectin

Ensure the fruit is in prime condition and remove any with blemishes. Place in a bowl and mash roughly using a fork. Add the sugar and leave to stand for half an hour. Add the pectin, stir well, then pour the jam into the prepared containers. I use a supply of yoghurt or plastic containers with lids. Allow this jam to stand for at least 3 hours in a cool place before placing the lids on top. Place in the fridge for at least 24 hours before freezing. Defrost before serving.

Bramble Jelly

It has taken me many years to acquire patience and now that I have, I am content to stand by and watch jams turning into jellies. This bramble jelly has a unique flavour of the countryside and if you can find elderberries, those pretty black berries from the elderflower tree, try combining them with blackberries for a really good preserve. Adjust the quantities to suit your fruit. Pick fruit which is not over-ripe.

1.80 kg (4 lb) blackberries
450 g (1 lb) elderberries } **total fruit = 2.25 kg (5 lb)**
570 ml (1 pint) water
Juice of 1 lemon
450 g (1 lb) sugar to each 570 ml (1 pint) fruit juice

Remove the berries from the stalks, wash and place in a preserving pan with the water and lemon juice. Simmer until soft and pulpy, then strain through a jelly bag. If you don't have a jelly bag use a sieve lined with muslin. Measure the fruit juice and the correct amount of warmed sugar back into the preserving pan and stir over a gentle heat until the sugar has dissolved; bring to the boil and boil rapidly until the jelly shows signs of setting. Pour into warm sterilised jars and cover.

To test for setting, place 1 dessertsp. of the jelly onto a plate, leave to cool, then if pressed with your finger the surface should wrinkle, indicating setting point has been reached.

Makes 3.15-3.60 kg (7-8 lb) jelly

Haw Jelly

This jelly is good to have in the jars at Christmas time. It goes particularly well with cold roast ham or turkey. Pick the haws when they are just ripe, removing any leaves or stalks. Wash well before using.

900 g (2 lb) haws
850 ml (1½ pints) water
Juice of 1 lemon and 1 lime
Granulated sugar, 450 g (1 lb) to each pint of juice

Simmer the washed haws in a pan with the water until soft and pulpy. Stir occasionally during cooking. Leave to cool slightly, then transfer to a jelly bag and allow the jelly to drip through. Do not attempt to speed up this process or the jelly will become cloudy. This may take 4-5 hours. Measure the liquid and for each pint of liquid add 450 g (1 lb) of granulated sugar. Add the lemon and lime juices. If you cannot find limes then lemons can be used on their own.

Place all the ingredients in a large heavy-based saucepan or preserving pan and allow the sugar to dissolve over a gentle heat. Then boil rapidly until setting point has been reached. Test 1 dessertsp. of jelly on a plate, allow to cool and if it shows signs of wrinkling when the plate is tipped, then the jelly is ready to bottle. Remove any scum which may appear on the surface before bottling in clean, sterile jars. Cover and store in a cool, dark cupboard.

Makes approximately 1.80 kg (4 lb) jelly

Traditional Orange Marmalade 'The Seville Way'

I have made endless varieties of marmalade yet I still come back to my favourite traditional orange marmalade made with that bitter variety of orange—the Seville—available from December to February.

900 g (2 lb) Seville oranges
2 lemons
1.7 L (3 pints) cold water
1.80 kg (4 lb) granulated or preserving sugar

Squeeze the juice from the oranges and lemons and place this juice in a large pan. Cut the peel only from the fruit shells, being careful not to include the pith as it spoils the flavour and colour of the finished marmalade. You may find it easier to remove the peel from the oranges before squeezing the juice from them. Cut the peel into fine shreds. This is time-consuming but well worth the effort. I like to make the peel very fine. Place the pips and centres of the squeezed oranges in a muslin bag and add to the pan with the peel. Add the water and simmer over a low heat until the peel has softened and the liquid has reduced by almost half.

At this stage, squeeze the muslin bag, allowing any juice to run into the pan. Add the sugar, stirring slowly until it has dissolved. Bring to the boil

121

and stir occasionally until setting point is reached, approximately 15 minutes, or try using the wrinkle test where a little marmalade is placed on a saucer and left to cool for a few minutes. If it wrinkles when tilted and forms a skin, then the marmalade is ready.

Allow the marmalade to cool slightly before putting in clean, sterile jars as this will distribute the peel evenly. Top with wax discs and when cold, cover and store in a dark cupboard.

Makes approximately 2.25-2.70 kg (5-6 lb) marmalade

Canadian Tomato Pickle

3.15 kg (7 lb) tomatoes
1 head celery
7 large onions
2 red and 2 green peppers
55 g (2 oz) mustard seeds
170 g (6 oz) salt
1.35 kg (3 lb) granulated sugar
280 ml (½ pint) white vinegar

The success of this recipe lies in the fine chopping of all ingredients and in keeping the vegetables roughly the same size.

Place all the chopped vegetables and mustard seeds in a bowl with the salt. Mix well, then place in a muslin or cheese cloth, tie up and allow to drain overnight.

In a saucepan dissolve the sugar in the heated vinegar and 140 ml (¼ pint) of the strained liquid. Allow to cool. Add the pulp of the vegetables. Stir and pot in sterile containers.

Makes approximately 4.50 kg (10 lb)

Windfall Pears in Port

This is an ideal way of coping with those pears that blow from the trees in early autumn before they are completely ripe. For this preserve choose pears that are not bruised. They may also be peeled.

900 g (2 lb) windfall pears

Syrup
850 ml (1½ pints) water
225 g (8 oz) granulated sugar
Juice of 1 lemon
70 ml (⅛ pint) port

Wipe the pears and pack tightly in kilner or preserving jars. Prepare the syrup, dissolving the sugar in the water and lemon juice. Bring to the boil and boil rapidly for 3 minutes. Add the port, mix well, then pour over the pears. Seal the jars but not completely until after cooking in the oven. Place on a baking sheet and cook in the oven at 180 °C (350 °F or regulo 4) for about 15 minutes, until the pears show signs of softening but still retain their shape. Remove from the oven and screw the tops securely on the jars.

These pears make a lovely instant winter pudding. Serve with nutmeg-flavoured whipped cream or yoghurt.

Sun-dried Tomatoes

At last a new way of coping with the glut of tomatoes: sun-dried tomatoes can be used in such a variety of recipes. I find the smaller tomatoes better for drying but choose them ripe and without blemishes.

15-20 ripe, firm tomatoes
115 g (4 oz) sea salt
Extra virgin olive oil

Dry the tomatoes, cut in half and place on trays with the cut side upper-most. Sprinkle a little salt over the cut half of each tomato. Cover with light trays or fine wire mesh to protect from insects while drying in the fresh air. Place the trays in a sunny position where they can be left for at least 4-5 days in warm sunny weather. Do not allow them to become damp in any way. Lift the wire mesh off the tomatoes twice each day, pressing gently down on the fruit with a spoon or your fingers to help the moisture rise to the surface and then evaporate. At the end of this process the tomatoes should be dry and wrinkled.

Pack into sterile jars, fill up with olive oil and seal the jars.

Preserved Lemon Slices

3-4 lemons
10-12 cloves
280 ml (½ pint) water
55 g (2 oz) sugar
Bay leaf

The number of lemons you require will depend upon the size of your jar. Choose small lemons with thin skins, cut into slices and stud with cloves. Pack tightly into kilner or screw-top jars and pour in the syrup mixture, which is made by bubbling the sugar and water together until dissolved. Add the bay leaf and seal the jars tightly. Serve with hot drinks. Perfect for spicing up a fish dish.

Candied Lime, Lemon and Orange Peel

Never throw away the peel of any citrus fruits as this can be candied so easily and the only ingredient needed is sugar.

3 lemons
3 limes
3 oranges
450 g (1 lb) granulated sugar

Peel the fruits removing as much pith as possible. Cut the peel into slices and boil in a saucepan of water, just sufficient to cover them, for approximately 45 minutes or until the peel becomes soft. Change the water in the pan and repeat this process, cooking for a further 15 minutes. Remove the peel from the pan and reduce the liquid down to approximately 280 ml (½ pint) by rapid boiling. Next add the sugar to the liquid, bring to the boil and remove from the heat. Add the strips of peel and push down well below the syrup. Place a lid on the pan and leave immersed in the syrup for 48 hours.

Reheat the peel and syrup mixture and cook for approximately 5 minutes. Drain the peel and leave on plates to cool until it no longer appears sticky. If being used for sweet dishes toss in caster sugar and store in air-tight jars. If for savoury use, store without dusting.

Lavender Lemonade

1.1 L (2 pints) water
225 g (8 oz) caster sugar
4 dessertsp. coarsely chopped lavender leaves
**   or 1 tablesp. dried lavender flowers**
570 ml (1 pint) water
140 ml (¼ pint) fresh lemon juice
55 g (2 oz) caster sugar

In a pan combine 1.1 L (2 pints) of water and 225 g (8 oz) of sugar. Bring to the boil and simmer until the sugar has dissolved. Remove from the heat and add the lavender leaves. Cover and leave aside to infuse for 2-3 hours, then strain.

Return the liquid to the pan, add a further 570 ml (1 pint) water, lemon juice and 55 g (2 oz) caster sugar. Re-heat until the sugar has dissolved, then cool.

To serve, pour into chilled glasses with ice cubes and several chopped strawberries. The strawberries are optional but they turn this unusual summery lemonade a pretty pink colour. Serve garnished with a slice of lemon and a sprig of lavender.

Index

apple sauce, 70

apples
    Apple Cordial, 116-17
    Baked Bramley Apples with Raisins and
        Hazelnuts, 87
    Blackberry and Apple Crêpes, 104-5
    Blackberry and Apple Pie, 86
    Bramley and Roasted Nut Cake, 87-8
    Bread and Apple Pudding, 89
    Hot Apple Cider, 92
    Stilton, Walnut and Apple Strudel, 113
    Toffee Apple Tart, 90-91
    Toffee Apples, 85
    Very Irish Potato Apple Cake, 91

Apricot and Almond Brulée, 75

Aromatic Prawns, 4

Aromatic Pumpkin, 57-8

artichokes
    Jerusalem Artichokes in a Cheesy Sauce,
        61

bacon
    Festive Bacon and Eggs, 49-50
    Hot Bacon Soufflé with Sun-dried
        Tomato Sauce, 8
    Mother McKeag's Bacon Muffins, 109-10
    Sweetcorn and Bacon Burgers, 49

Baked Bramley Apples with Raisins and
    Hazelnuts, 87

Banana Tea Bread, 107

Bananas, Lemon and Rum-baked, 79

Barbary Duck Breasts with Rhubarb and
    Redcurrant Sauce, 64-5

Barbecue Sauce, 64

beef
    My Burgers, 48-9
    Warming Winter Hot Pot, 39-40

Beekeeper's Cake with Nutmeg, 98-9

beetroot
    Spiced Gingered Beetroot, 60-61

Berry Berry Fresh Fruit Cake, 100-101

Berry Brulée, 75-6

biscuits
    Spiced Wholemeal Biscuits, 110

Bitter Sweet Cocktails, 6

Blackberry and Apple Crêpes, 104-5

Blackberry and Apple Pie, 86

Blackberry Mist, 80

Braised Hot Pickled Red Cabbage with
    Apples, 92

Bramble Jelly, 120

Bramley and Roasted Nut Cake, 87-8

Brandied Peaches, 78

bread
    Banana Tea Bread, 107
    Crunchy Savoury Loaf, 109
    Hot Cross Irish Soda Bread with Herbs,
        108-9
    scones, 105-6
    Soda Bread with Cinnamon and Apple,
        89-90

Bread and Apple Pudding, 89

Bread and Butter Pudding, 73-4

Bread Sauce, 67

butter
    Sharp Lemon and Chive Butter, 63

butterscotch, 100

cabbage
    Braised Hot Pickled Red Cabbage with
        Apples, 92
    Country Cabbage, 54-5

cakes
    Banana Tea Bread, 107
    Beekeeper's Cake with Nutmeg, 98-9
    Berry Berry Fresh Fruit Cake, 100-101
    Bramley and Roasted Nut Cake, 87-8
    Cinnamon Tea Cake, 99-100
    A Cracking Good Cake, 111-12
    Irish Freckled Tea Loaf, 107
    My Favourite Yoghurt Cake, 98
    My Wedding Cake, 102-3
    Our Farmhouse Fruit Cake, 96
    Roasted Hazelnut and Rhubarb Cake,
        101-2
    Simnel Cake, 94-5
    Speedy Date Cake, 108
    Victorian Lemon Cake with Elderflower
        and Lemon Curd, 97-8